A year OF
inner peace

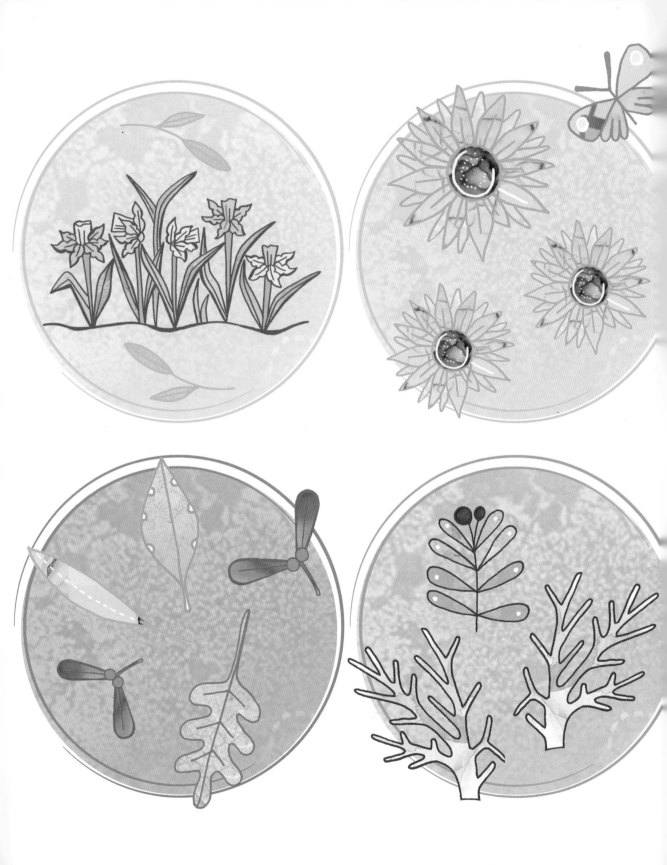

A year of inner peace

find a calmer and happier way of being

kirsten riddle

CICO BOOKS
LONDON NEW YORK

Published in 2024 by CICO Books
An imprint of Ryland Peters & Small Ltd

20–21 Jockey's Fields   341 E 116th St
London WC1R 4BW   New York, NY 10029

www.rylandpeters.com

10 9 8 7 6 5 4 3 2 1

A CIP catalog record for this book is available from
the Library of Congress and the British Library.

ISBN: 978-1-80065-343-6

Printed in China

Illustrator: Hannah Davies
Square frames by @Adobe Stock/Eva Speshneva

Editor: Kristy Richardson
Senior designer: Emily Breen
Art director: Sally Powell
Creative director: Leslie Harrington
Head of production: Patricia Harrington
Publishing manager: Carmel Edmonds

contents

introduction

Peace is different for everyone, and that is how it should be. You are an individual and the journey you take is unique.

This voyage of discovery will lead you into uncharted territory, but the good news is you don't need to pack a case or boost your carbon footprint. This journey only requires one thing—an open and enquiring mind. The path to peace is littered with lessons, as you will discover as you work your way through this book.

what does peace mean to you?

Say the word "peace" very slowly and let it linger upon your tongue. The elongated sound slips easily from your lips and rides upon the crest of a breath, exuding calm. Peace is the stillness that sits within your chest, the settled feeling of comfort and succor that once cushioned you in the womb. It is the translucence of air, the feather-light sensation that takes over as you drift idly into daydream. Peace can be

a lilting, uplifting experience, but it is also grounding at times—a weight that anchors you to the earth and allows you to bend and weave upon destiny's breeze. It is a place of power, a space where you can become engrossed in the moment and connect with your core passions. It is also "home" and everything that represents.

a seasonal approach

Peace is colored by the seasons, and fluctuates accordingly depending on the weather, the elements, and the turn of nature's wheel. At the height of summer, peace burns brightly and casts a heavy glow upon your brow but enter autumn and you will discover its subtle changes, as the light dims and the earth hardens in preparation for winter's arrival. Going within seems natural then, as the temperature drops and you snuggle up calm and content in your burrow, but before you know it, spring skips across the threshold and the slumbering serenity that you were accustomed to becomes a thing of the past. Once more you are imbued with hope, and the kind of calmness that comes with renewed vigor.

how to use this book

This book takes a seasonal approach to inner peace. Week by week, note each of these phases and the effect that they have on your well-being. The activities and rituals promote the flow of harmony and offer a moment of stillness and understanding, either every day, during the week, at the weekend, or both, depending on your schedule. Some activities span the length of the week and move into the weekend. These suggestions are meant to be savored and done a little at a time. Other exercises provide a soothing quick fix that you can call

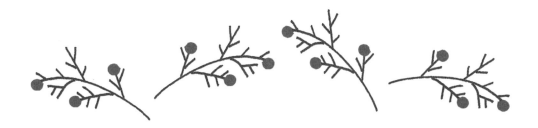

upon anytime. Some of the rituals can be repeated several times: others you only need to do once. Again, this is a personal choice. While each section has been carefully crafted to encompass different exercises and suggestions, it is up to you to navigate the weeks and choose the activities that feel right for you.

Within the pages you will find meditations, mindful moments, practical rituals, and journaling exercises to help you experience peace in its many guises. There are affirmations and mantras that you can repeat anytime during the week or month, and a seasonal, sensory focus to help you engage with your environment, wherever you are in the world. The book is written so that you can dip in at any point in the year and find calming tips and inspiration. The only thing you will need is a journal to help with some of the exercises and an eagerness to try something new—the rest is up to you and how you feel.

So why not start now? Turn the page and take a breath. Be kind to yourself and do not rush. Instead, engage fully with each experience and somewhere along the way peace will join you, slipping in quietly like an old friend, ready to soothe your heart and mind, and fill you with joy.

chapter 1

SPRING

spring's promise

Always a welcome relief after winter's long stay, spring may only be a heartbeat away and yet, at first, it's hard to see evidence of the season's takeover. We wait and wonder when the light will return. It is during this in-between state that we truly experience the gift of spring.

We look to a brighter future. We hope for warmer days. And slowly, as if in answer to our prayers, the changes come—but there is no rough and tumble, no race to the finish line, for spring is delicate in its footsteps. If anything, it meanders like a playful child taking its own sweet time to infuse the earth with warmth.

The ground, once hardened by winter's chilly grip, begins to soften beneath the sun's rays. Tendrils of light slip between the cracks, curling into the soil bed and whispering the promise of new life to the seeds and bulbs within. The grass, brittle and tired, begins to wake up, to feel the kiss of morning dew upon each blade, and the trees that once stood so stark and bare, skeletal in their wintry form, thicken and change color. The bark responds to the soothing warmth of the sun's touch, and slowly the branches come to life. What was once gnarly and exposed becomes youthful and strong. It is as if the land has been reborn, renewed by the wheel of time, which now turns in its favor.

"There's so much spring in the air—there's so much lazy sweetness in your heart."

F. Scott Fitzgerald

a gentle awakening

Like the plants, we too sense this shift. While it doesn't strike us like a thunderbolt, it stirs something deep within that we had almost forgotten—a lost childhood rolling around in the damp grass, sticky fingers lifting newly born flower heads for a deeper sniff, the gentle breeze giving us the fuel to fly or climb the nearest tree. It is all there in the arrival of spring. We are youthful once more, filled with a desire to create and make our mark. The same zest that stirs in the earth clings to our skin and seeps deeper, and we are suddenly aware of the force that moves within us.

Peace comes naturally with the sweep of the season, and in this case, it is a gentle awakening of mind and spirit. We are re-animated like the landscape, warmed through to our very core, leaving us open-hearted and ready for anything. Whether our desire is to climb the nearest mountain or sit

among the freshly formed buds and open the petals of our imagination through art or rhyme, we can find it here. If we need reminding of the power of love, then spring is the season to do that, for it reveals the true nature of beauty, which is neither showy nor demanding, but inspiring and uplifting. Calmness comes in the mellow trickle of a stream as it weaves a path through the undergrowth, and in the soft fragrance of wildflowers, early to rise and cluster together in the dense woodland. And even if we are not blessed with such floral delights, we can sense a thawing in other ways as the earth wakes up. Spring allows us to be still and appreciate its gifts, while feeling joyful about what is to come.

spring into a new season

It's no surprise that the word "spring" is used to describe this season, for there is a sense of wanting to leap out of those winter woollies and launch into something new. To cast off the old and jump for joy at the turning of the wheel. Perhaps it's the change in light that triggers this feeling, or maybe it's more subtle, something within us that stirs around the same time each year. Our internal clock works alongside the environment, and suddenly we feel renewed and ready to take on the world. Of course, for some, it's a little more sedate, like stepping purposely onto a bridge that transports you to a different place and time. With every footfall, the vista opens up and the sun shines a little brighter. The journey happens naturally, as if by magic, and before you know it spring has sprung!

Within this chapter you will discover how to tune into the buoyant wave of positive energy that's available. You will learn the secrets of spring, and how to tap into the source of its power and find the stillness you seek. The inner peace that you unearth is imbued with optimism, helping you to feel calm and positive in the face of challenges. You will ignite the creative spark within and use your imagination in new ways, which will inspire and fill you with confidence. You will experience the regenerative power of the season and how you can work with it to feel rejuvenated and recharged. You will learn to go with the flow, to look at life through an altogether more colorful lens, to begin to appreciate the wonder in your world, and how you are blessed with new beginnings and opportunities for growth every day. Most of all, you will see that peace can be found in playful moments shared with your nearest and dearest.

Peace is not only found in the realm of solitary silence seekers. Rather, it is everywhere—in each fresh sapling and flower that bursts into being, in every creature that walks the Earth, and those newly born to the planet. Spring will help you reconnect with your true nature and that in itself will bring a deeper sense of tranquility to your soul.

SPRING WATCH

If you only do one thing this spring, make a point of stepping out into the world. You don't have to set yourself a challenge. Instead, take your time and get moving with a gentle walk or some pottering in the backyard. Take a minute to look at your outside space and assess what needs doing. Open your mind and breathe in the fresh air, then clear away the debris of winter and prepare the earth for new life.

embrace renewal

Spring represents a new beginning—this season is a chance to begin again, and to plant the seeds for future success.

Skeletal shrubs take on new life, with plump shoots and an abundance of leaves. The grass begins to grow once more. The animals of the Earth wake up and make merry because they know this is their chance to recharge and thrive.

In ancient times, there were many ways to mark the beginning of spring. From rites and rituals to simple prayers of thanks, the people made the effort to acknowledge the change in seasons. You can do the same and embrace spring's vibrant energy by stepping into your power and implanting key intentions. In doing so, you cement your connection with the natural world and promote a sense of inner peace and confidence.

To begin setting a few spring intentions, you'll need some time to establish exactly how you'd like to feel and what you want to achieve (see opposite). Once you have planted the seeds of intention, they will soon blossom into action!

MANTRA FOR THE WEEK:

"Spring fills me with anticipation!"

this week SEEDS OF INTENTION

Set some time aside when you won't be disturbed to establish some springtime intentions. You can do this outside in the backyard or looking out of a window—a view of the natural world can promote positive emotions and inspire you. You will need a pen and your journal.

Monday: Consider how you feel right now. In your journal, write a few words that occur to you at the bottom of the page (for example, "tired", "hopeful," "bored," and so on). Sit with your thoughts and reflect.

Tuesday: Return to your words of the previous day. Just above them, draw a line going upward like the stem of a plant and leave some space at the top where the flower head would be. In this space write how you would like to feel as you blossom. You might say "energized," "confident," or "excited."

Wednesday: Spend today thinking about any aspirations you have for the future. For example, perhaps you'd like to complete a marathon or find a new job. Add these ideas to the blossoming flower at the top of your journal.

Thursday: Today, think about the things that you could do in the next few weeks or months that might help you reach the goals in your journal. For example, "build some regular exercise into my routine" or "challenge myself to learn something new." Add these along the stem of your bloom.

Friday: Look back at what you have written in your journal this week and observe how your intentions have grown. Read your words out loud, and at the end, add *"This spring I step into my power and welcome positive change."*

At the weekend: Write down how you feel about the coming weeks and months in your journal. You might even feel like taking action on some of the steps that will help you reach your goals.

lighter days

Spring marks the beginning of the seasonal wheel of the year, and while it can be hard to define exactly when it starts, we see the light return to the earth.

With the entrance of spring, the sun, which may have seemed distant over the winter months, now makes a reappearance. Not fully in its prime, it emits a gentle warmth and brightness, and brings a tinge of color to the landscape.

The sun is a blessing that we can all benefit from. It provides much-needed vitamin D, which is in low supply after all those winter months being tucked away inside. The generous light it brings not only heals and restores the spirit, but also helps to strengthen bones, lower blood pressure, and lift the mood, improving mental health. You will also sleep better because the light helps to regulate your body's internal rhythm and boosts the sleep-promoting hormone melatonin.

greet the day

You can treat each new day as the first of the season. Welcome the day as you would an old friend. If you think of it in this way, then the moment you rise is a chance to start again, to emerge into the light and make your mark.

While you might not feel like leaping out of bed, take a minute to engage with the world by taking a deep breath. Let the air filter through your body as you gently position your feet upon the ground. Feel the connection to the earth and stand, letting your weight drop down into your lower legs. Once up, spread your arms wide in a welcoming gesture, and smile. Say *"Hello world, hello new day!"*

step into the light

Everything looks and feels better in the sunshine. You might not have time to sit and soak up the sun this week, but you can benefit by making a point of going outside for at least five minutes every day. Try these tips to make the most of your time in the sun:

- As you go about your business, imagine breathing in the sunshine. While you walk to and from the store or to work, feel the light hit the top of your head, travel down your spine, and into your chest.

- A stroll around the backyard or a walk to the end of your drive is enough to experience the warmth of the sun. Focus on the warmth you feel throughout your body, paying attention to each muscle and limb.

- No matter the weather, spend a few moments in meditation focusing on the mantra *"I let my light shine!"*

- Imagine that with every breath you take, you become lighter and brighter as you absorb the sunshine.

- Picture the sun's rays casting a spotlight over you.

- At the end of the day, stand for a moment in the waning sunlight and feel the weight of the day shift from your shoulders. Let the sun's soothing rays melt away any tension.

hear the call of spring

Connecting with nature is guaranteed to promote peaceful feelings and help you to de-stress. One of the best ways to do this is to physically connect through your senses.

Sniffing a flower, hugging a tree, or listening to birdsong, for example, will give you the chance to experience your surroundings fully. In the same way, connecting with family and friends and the people we love through our senses is guaranteed to give us a boost.

A chat on the telephone is a great way to connect and feel good. But how well can you really listen? Listening is a skill and a key part of communication. If you can learn to listen to others (see opposite), then you will listen to yourself and what your body and mind is telling you more effectively. You will also feel the benefit of listening to the silence, which can help to maintain inner peace.

sing nature's song

At this time of the year, it feels like everything is waking up. The earth is stirring and there's an air of anticipation everywhere. One of the earliest signs of spring is the dawn chorus. The sound of birdsong first thing in the morning is a beautiful alarm call, and a herald of the joy to come.

Take some time to listen to the melody of the birds. If you're already up, simply stop what you're doing and give yourself a minute or two to follow the notes. If you're usually in bed, make a point of setting your alarm a bit earlier so that you can catch the birds performing. Close your eyes and identify the different sounds, and let the tune fill your head. Drift away, letting the harmony infuse you with serenity and hope for the day.

sensory LISTEN WITH INTENT

Listening, like any skill, takes practice. You may think that you are an expert, but when another person is speaking how much do you really take in? If you were to challenge yourself to recall every part of the conversation, would you be able to remember exactly what was said? More importantly, are you able to look between the words and sentences and sense what the other person is feeling?

During conversations this week, make a point of trying these steps, which should help you remain present and listen with intent.

Step 1: Make a point of sitting down with a friend or family member and asking how they feel. Ask what is going on in their life right now, then be still and listen. You can also do this with work colleagues.

Step 2: Let the person speak and encourage them with prompts and questions. Look the person in the eye every so often, as this will reassure them that you are listening. Resist the urge to interrupt.

Step 3: Listen to the inflection of their voice—the tone and speed with which they speak. There will be clues in the way they present themselves and how they talk. For example, if someone takes their time, they're thinking deeply about what they want to say. This could be because there is something on their mind, or they want to present themselves in a certain way. If someone talks quietly, this could indicate that they're feeling vulnerable. If they become animated, then they're obviously excited or emotionally charged.

Step 4: If you find your mind wandering, bring yourself back to the present moment and focus on the tone and expression of the voice.

Step 5: Listen to the words and build a picture in your mind of what you hear, then respond accordingly.

pause

One of the best ways to feel instantly Zen is to take notice and be in the present moment. The good news is that spring is a wonderful season to do this. There is so much to see and so many changes to note that you won't be short of inspiration.

It's not always easy to pause when you're rushing through your day, but you can get into the habit of being present automatically if you make it a part of your routine. All you have to do is stop what you are doing completely and focus on what is right in front of you.

practice paying attention

Choose a time that suits you and stick to it. For example, mid-morning when you have your cup of coffee, at lunchtime, or perhaps later in the day when you feel the mid-afternoon tiredness hit. If you're inside, perhaps in an office, look out of the window. Alternatively, turn your attention to something indoors—for example, the smell of coffee brewing, the sound of your colleagues chattering, or the gentle rumble of traffic outside. Engage each one of your senses and see what stands out. Fix your attention on this for a minute and breathe. If it helps you to focus, perhaps tell yourself: *"I am present, in the now, and open to new experiences."*

spring showers

Spring showers come thick and fast. They may not last long, but a downpour can be sudden and unexpected. Rather than resist the uncomfortable or unexpected, try to go with the flow.

Being flexible, whether in mind or body, is a skill. Once mastered, it will help you feel at peace. Rather than resisting friction, you learn to work with it and use it to your advantage, which helps to restore balance. So, take inspiration from these impromptu gifts of nature. Don't resist the water, embrace it!

Water has the ability to flow where it is needed, moving around and over obstacles and adapting to the environment. Take inspiration from this and learn to be flexible like the rain that washes over the land (see page 25).

sip and savor

Those torrents of rain sent from the heavens are much needed by the earth, which has for a time struggled under the weight of winter's harshness. Rain helps to soften and quench the soil, feeding the thirst of those hungry little saplings waiting to blossom. You, too, can stay hydrated to calm a whirling mind.

Drinking water regularly helps the brain produce serotonin (also known as the feel-good chemical). Take regular water breaks throughout the day and try to increase your water intake by at least one or two glasses.

Focus on the taste and feel of water in your mouth and allow your mind to take a break from other thoughts. You'll soon notice that just a minute taken to sip water can bring you peace and renewed energy.

sensory SHOWER POWER

Learn to dance in the rain! You don't have to walk far in a downpour—
if you want, you can simply stand outside in your backyard and experience
the same benefits. Just make sure to have a good rain mac and appropriate
footwear to keep your feet dry. Then follow these steps.

Step 1: Imagine you're standing in your own shower—the only difference is
you're fully clothed and outside. Breathe deeply and turn your face upward
for a few seconds.

Step 2: Close your eyes and concentrate on the feel of the raindrops against
your skin. Relax and stand there for a couple more minutes. Let the rain hit
the top of your head, and as it splashes to the ground, imagine that each
cleansing drop is washing away any negative thoughts and feelings. You
might want to say out loud: *"I am replenished and refreshed!"*

Step 3: Engage your hearing and listen to the sound of the rainfall. Let this
be a kind of background music to soothe your soul.

Step 4: Enjoy the sensation of the rain as it trickles over your face and
hands. Feel it wash away any stress you have been carrying. Breathe
deeply and relax.

visualization WOODLAND STREAM

This visualization is one of the easiest ways to practice flexibility. At any point in your day when you're faced with an obstacle, remind yourself of the woodland stream.

Take a deep breath and transport yourself to a forest. Imagine that you are fluid and free-flowing, a part of the gentle flow of water that curls its way through the undergrowth. It doesn't try to force its way through the rocks because that would be impossible. Instead, it flows over and around them to create a new thread of water. You move with the landscape. Where will you go next? How can you work with the obstacle to achieve your aim?

Give your body a gentle shake and stretch to alleviate any stress, then let your mind wander.

choose happiness

Spring, with all its new growth and lighter, brighter days, is naturally aligned with harmony. There are plenty of reasons to feel joyful at this time of the year.

With this in mind, take your lead from your environment and take some time to feel happy. Remember—happiness is not something that happens to you, but an inner feeling of deep contentment that you can call upon at any time.

this week **PLAY A GAME**

As we get older, we put aside childish ways. Our imagination, which was at the forefront of many childhood games, takes a back seat and we become focused on more mundane concerns. This is only natural, and part of growing up and becoming an adult. That said, there's something fun in going back in time and playing some of those games that you enjoyed when you were younger. It helps you reconnect with your inner child and provides pleasure in its simplest form. Soothe away anxiety throughout the week by being playful, and you will feel a deep well of peace within.

Monday: What makes you happy at the moment? Take some time today to think about the things you enjoy and what you like to do. Write them down in your journal to remember the following day.

Tuesday: Today, list three games or things that you loved to do as a child. Remember simple playground games, making up stories and acting them out, or perhaps something active, like rollerblading or climbing trees.

Wednesday: Compare the lists in your journal. You might notice there are overlaps between what you enjoy now and what you loved doing as a child. It might be the opposite and you have nothing in common with your childhood games. Look at your favorite games and next to each one, write a word that sums up how this activity made you feel—for example, "free" or "adventurous."

MANTRA FOR THE WEEK:

"My inner child reminds me to have fun and 'play' worries away."

Thursday: Today, pick one of the items from your list and set aside a time to do it. Be practical and choose something that will not only make you feel good but is also easy for you to do. If you're seeing friends or spending time with family during the day, you might choose a ball game that you can play in the backyard. Alternatively, if you're going to be on your own in the evening, you might decide to make up a story or paint a picture.

Friday: Think back to yesterday's activity and notice how you feel. Pay attention to any changes in mood or energy. Enjoy taking a wander back in time, connect with the child you once were, and bring some of that wonder into your world today.

At the weekend: Stop regularly throughout the weekend and focus on one thing that makes you feel good. This could be something you see outside or from your window, or something in your home like a pretty plant or even your pet cat or dog. It could be something that is working for you in the moment; for example, you're in the flow with friends or family, or perhaps you are feeling particularly creative. Acknowledge the things that make you happy and feel the joy.

stop to smell the roses

Flowers have a way of making us feel good. With an uplifting scent and a beauty that is unique to each bloom, they are a gift from nature and a reminder that individuality is a blessing.

Take a moment to consider how wildflowers grow, springing up from the earth wherever they can, with little effort from human hands. These flowers respond to the elements and flourish in their own time. There is no rush here. Everything happens when it happens, and the result is a sea of beauty that we can enjoy. There is something peaceful about the flower's journey to fruition. Gazing at its beauty can help us reconnect with the natural world and imbue us with inner calm.

say it with flowers

Flowers are a wonderful gift that are sure to heal any rift, put a smile on someone's face (including your own), and brighten the home. Yellow is the sunshine shade. It's associated with joy, friendship, and a zest for life. Combine the two and invest in a bunch of yellow flowers. Opt for blooms that are in abundance at this time of year. Tie with a red ribbon and give them as a gift to someone you love.

MANTRA FOR THE WEEK:

"Like a flower, I grow in strength and beauty every day."

sensory THE FIVE SENSES

Being in the moment means engaging all of your senses. We tend to rely heavily on one at a time. For example, we might concentrate on what we can see rather than what we can smell or hear. The other senses become backup senses, so we don't use them to their full potential.

To create a sense of calm or to de-stress, try this step-by-step exercise when you have plenty of time to explore each sense. You will need access to a backyard or a park with lots of plants or flowers. A planter with flowering blooms is also perfect for this exercise.

Step 1: Home in on a flower. A rose is the perfect choice, as it has so many layers to its beauty, but if you prefer you can choose a different type of bloom.

Step 2: Spend some time simply appreciating the flower. Look at its size, shape, and color, and consider any striking features. What do you like about how it looks? Can you see any intricate details or patterns? Is there anything that makes this flower stand out to you?

Step 3: Engage your sense of smell and inhale the sweet fragrance. What does it remind you of?

Step 4: Gently cup the flower head in your hands. How does it feel to touch?

Step 5: What can you hear as you examine the flower? You might notice a bee humming nearby or birdsong in the distance.

Step 6: Be entranced by the beauty of the bloom and take in as much detail as you can, but also enjoy the experience. Let your focus be solely on the flower and take your time. In doing so, you should feel a wave of tranquility settle over you. Breathe in the joy of each flower and savor a moment of peace in their company.

breathe

The way you breathe has a direct effect on your mental well-being and your ability to stay calm and balanced.

If you breathe correctly, you take in the right amount of oxygen, which in turn slows your heart rate. The more oxygen you are able to take in, the more relaxed and at peace you will feel. Get into the habit of checking in with your breathing throughout the day. It only takes a minute and it's well worth the effort, as you will start to notice when you are holding on to your breath, or shallow breathing.

visualization LOOP

Stop what you are doing and notice how your chest feels. If it feels tight or tense, it may help to deepen your breath with this quick visualization.

Take a long, slow breath in. Imagine you are drawing it from the base of your spine, up the length of your back and neck, and over the top of your head. Feel the air inflate your chest. Say *"I make room for me to breathe."*

As you exhale, follow the journey of the breath in a loop, which travels down into your lower belly and then back to the base of your spine ready to go again.

Continue this breathing cycle, taking your time as you go. Repeat for a minute and then carry on with your day.

a spring clean

With the coming of the sun, there is a feeling of expansion. Spring provides space for you to discard unwanted items, and that includes emotions and other beliefs that no longer serve a purpose. Spring-clean your life, as you would your home, to help you feel more at peace and balanced.

It makes sense that what we see on the outside reflects how we feel on the inside. For example, when we feel stressed, we're likely to put things down or toss them to one side, creating more clutter because our minds are full. Our focus is elsewhere, and because of this, our environment suffers. The reverse is also true. If your home is a mess, the sight of all the clutter is likely to make you feel closed in and tense. A clear, tidy room will give you space to think, breathe, and maneuver. Space in your environment equals space in your mind, making you less likely to feel stressed.

bin the burden

As you go about your daily routine, you will gather rubbish in the form of negative thoughts and feelings. As much as you try to stay positive and centered, it's inevitable that you will pick up residual energy. A bit like an ornament gathering dust, you can't help but absorb feelings and tensions that will have an impact on your personal peace.

Eliminate these things as you would the trash. Spend a couple of minutes at the end of the day thinking of anything that has been bothering you. If you can't pinpoint something directly, think about how you feel—for example, "tired" or "tense" and write that down on a piece of paper. Screw it up into a ball and throw it in the trashcan. This physical action will help you release the emotional baggage, and you should feel a little lighter.

this weekend CLEAR THE CLUTTER

All you need for this exercise is a bit of time, some paper, pens, and colored pencils, a journal where you can reflect, and an open heart and mind.

Step 1: Spread a sheet of paper out on a table or desk in front of you. Draw a large box to fill most of the sheet. This box represents your life.

Step 2: Break the box into smaller-sized boxes to signify different areas of your life—for example, family, work, friends, hobbies, fitness, self-care, and so on. Try to give each segment a space that reflects how much time you devote to it, so if you tend to bring your work home, let that show in the size of the box you give it.

Step 3: Look at the diagram you have created and see if there is any way that you can give yourself more room to breathe or some space for yourself. For example, you might have a box dedicated to outside commitments, like committees or groups that you no longer have time for, or don't enjoy anymore. If this is the case, block the box out by coloring it in. Which boxes could you get rid of altogether?

Step 4: Are there any boxes you could reduce? Write down any thoughts that you have in your journal. This will help you come up with a future plan to move the boxes around. Once you begin reducing the amount of time and energy that you give to unwanted boxes, you allow calmness in and give yourself the space and freedom to relax, which in turn creates a peaceful environment.

Step 5: Keep the diagram in easy reach so that you can refer to it daily. Remind yourself to clear the clutter and find some room to breathe.

visualization SPRING-CLEAN YOUR AURA

The aura is the energy field that sits around your body, almost like a picture frame encasing you in light. It can be many different colors, depending on how you feel. For example, a rosy tint to your aura might suggest you're in a loving mood, while purple could show you're feeling intuitive. The brightness of your aura is also affected by your mood, and if you've been suffering with stress or anxiety this can block the flow of energy, which leaves you even more depleted. To keep your aura in tip-top condition, it's important to have a spring-clean. This exercise can help to flush out negativity, which in turn will make you feel positive, energized, and at peace with yourself and the world.

Step 1: Fill a small bowl with hot water and add either a handful of fresh sage leaves or several drops of sage essential oil. Position the bowl nearby, so that you can smell the sage-infused vapors.

Step 2: Stand with your feet hip-width apart. Relax your shoulders and lengthen your spine. Breathe deeply and inhale the fresh scent.

Step 3: With your hands, or with a small makeup brush if you have one, flick the space that surrounds you. Imagine you're brushing away any debris from your aura. Begin at the top of your head and continue down, along your neck, shoulders, arms, and around your chest and stomach, then along each leg and foot.

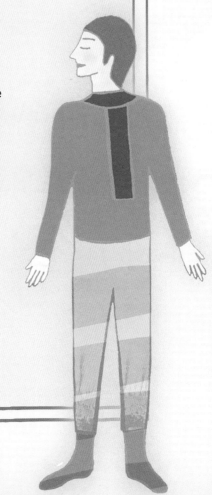

Step 4: Inhale the sage fragrance, taking it deep within your chest. As you exhale, imagine all the negative energy you have collected slipping from your aura.

Step 5: When you have finished, stand for a moment and picture your aura. Imagine it shining brightly like a golden cloak of light that surrounds you.

the magic of spring

There is wonder in everything, and it's easy to see it at this point in the year. You can experience nature's magic for yourself just by watching the plants and flowers grow, and the animals emerge from their winter sleep. New life is born, and the landscape is filled with potential.

Your life mirrors that of the natural world because we move in sequence with the rhythm of the season. Even if you've never been aware of this before, now is the time to recognize your part in the wheel of the year, and to embrace the magic of rebirth.

Set an intention to see the world with new eyes. As you go about your daily tasks, take a deep breath and acknowledge *"There is magic in everything I see and do."*

Like nature, you are reborn at this time of year. This is a new cycle, which you can make your own. Embrace the power of rebirth by releasing the past with love. Open your heart, see the world afresh, and you will discover the magic of this season.

this week SEE THE WONDER

This week, make a point of recognizing the magic in the world by pretending to be a tourist in your own life. Imagine, as you go about your days, that you are seeing everything for the first time. It might be difficult to get into this mindset but keep practicing. Once you get into the habit of doing it, you will begin to see how magical your life is and you can carry this mindset through the year.

Monday: Imagine as you drink your morning brew that this is the first time you have tasted it. Savor the experience.

Tuesday: Today, pretend your home is new to you. See it through the eyes of someone else and recognize all the good things that you take for granted. Notice how comfortable and welcoming it is, take in all the items you have collected, and what each one means.

Wednesday: Look at the outside world—the places you usually visit like the local park or store. As you walk, take in your surroundings and imagine that this is the first time you have done this. What do you notice about the experience?

Thursday: At the gym, pretend you have never been there before, and look through the eyes of a stranger at all the fantastic equipment. How does the experience of working out make you feel?

Friday: Going for dinner with friends? Revel in each moment and take joy from your surroundings and the delicious food. Imagine it's the first time you have tasted anything from the menu and relish the experience.

At the weekend: Look at yourself with fresh eyes. Scroll through recent photos and see them as a stranger would. Notice the emotion and joy on your face, and how beautiful and individual you look. Gaze at your reflection as if for the first time and recognize your worth.

nurture and grow

Spring is all about new beginnings, sowing the seeds for the future and setting things in motion that will hopefully bear fruit in the summer months.

Getting out into the fresh air and connecting with nature at a deeper level has been proven to improve the mood, balance the emotions, and soothe the spirit. Working with the land and watching the fruits of your labors eventually

this weekend GO WILD

The process of planting and tending to flowers is nurturing. It imbues you with a sense of peace and achievement—plus, doing your bit for the environment is a wonderful way to calm the mind.

You don't need a lot of space, or even a backyard, to grow your own plants. Even if you don't have outside space, a large pot can be used to sow seeds. A medium-sized planter with holes in the bottom can be used to grow a selection of plants or vegetables.

Herbs are a great addition to any kitchen and can be used in meals or to make calming and uplifting teas. While you can buy them from the grocery store, nothing beats

harvesting your own. Sage, thyme, rosemary, and oregano are the perfect bedfellows, encouraging each other to grow without taking over, while mint is best grown in its own pot as it demands lots of space. Alternatively, you could help pollinators like bees and butterflies by planting a wildflower meadow in your backyard.

Step 1: Outline your plot, however small. Choose an area that is exposed to the sun as this will help your flowers to grow. Once you have your space, rake through the soil to get rid of any weeds or stones or, if you are using pots, fill two-thirds of each planter with a peat-free compost.

Step 2: Using a trowel or your fingers, dig out a hole a little larger than the rootball. Position the young plant in the hole, then

blossom is rewarding. It will improve your long-term patience as well as your mental health!

Spring is a time, too, for making plans with friends and family. Nurture your relationships—and nurture yourself—by growing a network of loving alliances that you can call upon. Knowing that there are people out there who care for you will boost your inner peace.

fill with the remaining compost and gently pat the soil in place. Try to plant each one a hand's-width from the next, to give them room to breathe and flourish.

Step 3: Once you have planted all your plants, water well. If you have used pots, position the planters in the sun. Some herbs, like basil or coriander, don't thrive in too much sun, so pop the planter somewhere that gets a little sun for part of the day. If you have sown seeds, give them a good covering of water and continue to hydrate regularly, particularly through drier periods. Keep tending to your flowers and removing any weeds that grow around them.

Step 4: Enjoy the process! Nature cannot be rushed; it moves at its own pace and urges us to slow down and appreciate each tiny change. Harvest your herbs a little at a time, which gives the new leaves a chance to grow and flourish. Be patient and mindful as you watch the seeds grow into tiny shoots. Spend time in the coming weeks sitting near the area so that you can appreciate the surrounding wildlife. Eventually the blooms will spring to life, and you will have a place that you can go and drink in the beauty of nature.

herbal brew

If you're not a fan of using herbs in cooking, why not make your own herbal brew? This gives you the perfect opportunity to switch off and take a moment for yourself. Being caffeine-free, most herbal teas are calming, but you can enhance their healing effects by adding a spoonful of honey, which also has soothing properties. How you make your brew is as important as the time you spend sipping it. Take your time—treat it as a sacred ceremony and a moment for you to completely disengage from the world.

Rinse a handful of the fresh leaves, pop them in a cup or pan, and cover with boiling water. After at least five minutes of infusing, use a strainer to decant the tea, then pour the tea into a fresh cup. If you're adding honey, stir gently at first in a clockwise motion and then counterclockwise. Inhale the aroma of the scented steam before you taste.

Take a minute to appreciate the cup of tea you have made. As you lift it to your lips, acknowledge that **"the Earth nourishes and soothes my body and soul."** Notice the warmth beneath your fingers. Take a sip and let the liquid rest upon your tongue. Pay attention to the taste before you swallow. Breathe, and feel the stillness settle around you.

reach out

If peace is your goal this spring, then your relationships with your nearest and dearest should be near the top of your list. It isn't always easy to stay in touch with family and friends. While social media can certainly help you keep track of their movements, nothings beats a one-to-one conversation. Make an effort to connect with those that are important to you by having regular chats. A quick phone call—or even five minutes to have a cup of tea or herbal brew—makes all the difference. It shows you care and you're there—a practice which will be reciprocated over time.

a new beginning

Nature gets a chance to start again during the spring. New beginnings abound, and there is opportunity for reinvention.

Connect with spring's inspiring energy and set some time aside to reflect on where you are in life. Doing so will soothe your mind of worry, restore balance, and help you look to the future with optimism.

visualization REFLECT ON THE FUTURE

Try this mirror meditation to visualize your best self and imagine a bright future.

Step 1: Find a comfortable spot to sit, preferably outside so that you can reconnect with nature. Let your mind wander.

Step 2: Picture yourself standing in front of a mirror gazing at your reflection. Imagine that the image before you is the version that is your "best" self.

Step 3: See the reflection shimmer with light and love and acknowledge that you have the power to shine. You can be this person in the mirror—you can stand in your power and feel amazing. Remember that this is a new beginning and a chance to reinvent yourself and your life.

Step 4: Breathe and relax. Open your eyes and be excited for the future.

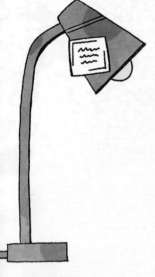

the power of words

The words you choose to use on a daily basis affect how you feel and the energy you put out into the world.

If your words are tinged with negativity, then your energy will be depleted and according to the law of attraction, you will draw more of the same to you. If your words are positive and imbued with peace and harmony, then you will attract the same kind of energy into your life.

To maintain positive energy and keep a calm and open mind, you need to be present and aware of your thinking patterns. This can be difficult when you're faced with a stressful situation. If you feel under threat or anxious, you'll naturally go into fight-or-flight mode, and it's likely you will lose yourself in a spiral of negative thoughts.

sticky note quotes

To combat negativity, train your brain to focus on the positive. Arm yourself with uplifting and soothing quotes. Choose a handful of your favorites—the ones that really resonate with you and make you feel calm—and write them on colorful sticky notes. Position them around your area of work, in diaries, notebooks, and even in your pockets. Consider these your weapons in the fight against stress. Like candles, crystals, and other calming tools, inspiring quotes can help to shift your mindset and restore balance.

MANTRA FOR THE WEEK:

"Every day is an opportunity to be creative and express myself."

this weekend **FIND YOUR INNER BARD**

When you are creative and use language imaginatively, you imbue your words with magic. You instantly feel inspired, uplifted, and calm. Take time to nourish this creative side of your personality. As you practice this type of writing, you'll notice your creativity flourishes and you'll find new outlets and ways to express yourself.

Step 1: Set some time aside when you are sure you won't be disturbed. Turn off your phone, the TV, and give yourself a break from technology; this will help the flow of your creativity.

Step 2: Begin writing about how you feel, so you might say: "Today I am feeling ... hopeful, excited, tired," and so on. Describe why you feel that way. Did something trigger these feelings? Perhaps earlier events caused you to feel like this. If so, write something about them.

Step 3: Describe where you are or, if you prefer, write about where you'd like to be, daydream a little, and have fun with this. Let your thoughts influence the pen. You don't have to write a massive amount; a few sentences is fine.

Step 4: Look at what you have written. Does anything jump out at you? Are there any key descriptive words that catch your eye? Could you put these in a short rhyme or poem to capture what you are feeling right now? If you feel inspired, have a go.

chapter 2

SUMMER

celebrate summer

The sweetness of spring soon slips from our memory as summer makes an entrance. She comes with a fanfare of color and warmth and demands our attention, taking center stage upon the Earth, like a carnival queen. She is resplendent and ready to inspire with a riot of hues at her fingertips.

Sometimes summer takes a softer approach, gradually filtering into view, curling golden rays of light between the drapes to tempt us out of our beds and to our feet. Her warmth is energizing as it seeps into the skin, easing weary bones and soothing aching ligaments, illuminating the core and easing heartache. Summer is an elixir which promises youth and vitality if you will only step into the light.

a riot of color

The land, too, benefits from the touch of summer, responding in kind to reveal an inner glow. Like a child cajoled and bathed in love, it visibly brightens, reaching upward for more. It instinctively knows that the season is here to nurture and entertain. The flowers, which have been waiting for her presence, open up and drink in her affection. Their petals extend outward to

"Rest is not idleness, and to lie sometimes on the grass under trees on a summer's day, listening to the murmur of the water, or watching the clouds float across the sky, is by no means a waste of time."

John Lubbock

reveal the beating heart of the bloom, and the scent that sings from each flower head draws new admirers. Gossamer-winged butterflies dance to the tune of summer, and rejoice at her return, for it is beneath the sun that they finally find succor. Bees, too, enjoy the vibrant seasonal energy, their wings vibrating as they go about their business, drawn by the beauty of each newly opened bloom and the nectar that hides within. Trees seem to stand ever taller, enjoying their moment in the spotlight. A symbol of strength and power, it is their time to flourish. And so the mutual adoration goes on, as summer blends with the environment in her unique way.

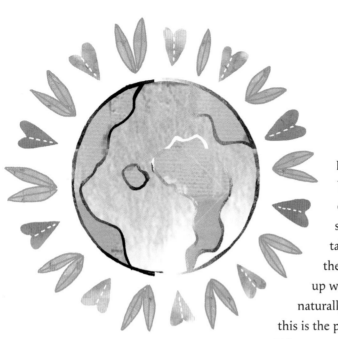

Remember, this is the vacation season. Whether you're going away to sunnier climes or treating yourself to a staycation, it's important to stop, take some time out for yourself, and let the vitality of your surroundings fill you up with joy. Self-pampering may not come naturally, but it's vital to your well-being, and this is the perfect point of the year to focus on you. Take your cue from wildlife and use this time to have fun and restore body and soul.

It is at the pinnacle of the year that peace is abundant. Even in the heaviest heat, a stillness can be found, for while the warmth may have weight which presses down upon your brow, it has a lesson too. It urges you to linger, to give in to the moment, and cease rushing, saying: "Relax, measure your breath while you can, and revel in each minute." There is no need for haste when summer's charms abound. This is the season to dawdle, to take a lengthy approach to everything. Regard the fiery orb that illuminates the sky as your personal charger and absorb those rays deeply. Open your heart and mind to the serenity of the sun and let it fill you with buoyancy. Do not rush to use it up—this is your chance to recharge and let the season calm your soul. Take your lead from the landscape, which is not hurried by the light but restored to its full potential. Lean back and let the earth support you, and make the most of each day of brightness, for like anything in life, it will not last forever.

relax, recharge, revitalize

On the following pages, you will learn how to work with the revitalizing energy of this season. You will discover how summer can help you relax to the very core of your being. Even if the heat is intense, you will find tranquility by doing simple techniques and exercises to slow body and mind and enjoy the stillness. You will reap the benefits of being outside, as and

when it is safe, and how to channel the power of the sun to fuel your dreams and desires. You will discover a renewed enthusiasm for each day, and you will learn to see the beauty in yourself, which in turn brings out the beauty in others. Summer can help you shine your light with confidence, while bringing a deeper sense of peace and acceptance. As you work on your self-esteem, you will experience the harmony that comes from being comfortable in your own skin and knowing who you are. This will carry you forward and create a sense of balance. You will embrace the freedom of the season and be able to enjoy nature's gifts, which in turn will help you feel content. Summer, and all that it brings, offers you the opportunity to unwind and loosen any shackles that have been holding you in place. It is your time to grow and glow.

SUMMER WATCH

If you only do one thing this summer, ensure you take plenty of time out to rest and absorb the glorious rays of the sun. Most of us spend the year rushing around in a whirl of activity, but this is the chance to step off that wheel and do something for you. Restoring yourself means you help others too, because rest helps you to become more effective and dynamic. So, have an afternoon siesta, read that book, or treat yourself to some beauty pampering.

wake up to summer

There's something joyful and serene about watching the sunrise. Being present in that moment, when the rising sun heralds the start of the day, is a gift of nature.

A sunrise is a sacred moment in time that you can share with nature and also an opportunity for you to be still and present. A sunrise is not something to be hurried or slotted in between other tasks.

It's not always possible to witness this marvel at other times of the year, especially when you have other commitments and you're working to a schedule. But in the summer, when the sun rises so early, you can make time to be part of the dawn of a new day.

this weekend WATCH THE SUN RISE

Set your alarm and prepare what you need the night before. You might want to take a blanket with you, and a pen and journal.

On the morning of the sunrise, choose a spot with a view. This could be in your backyard, local park, or on a hill out in the countryside. Sit, make sure you are comfy, and relax. Let your surroundings inspire you. This is the perfect time to set intentions for the day or even the month ahead, which you can write in your journal.

As the sun begins to rise, notice how it lights up the sky and brings the landscape to life. See the different colors and notice, too, any sounds. Perhaps you can hear the birds tweeting in the distance or the gentle rustle of tiny creatures in the undergrowth.

Pay attention to your breathing. Inhale the sweetness of a fresh new day and say *"I am filled with light and love."* Let the stillness settle in your chest as you connect with nature.

visualization TURN UP THE WARMTH

If you're lucky you'll see some sunshine during the summer months and that will put a positive and soothing spin on each day. Even if you don't, you can still feel the warmth within by turning up your inner glow. This is a simple technique that you can do at any point during the day when you need a positive boost, or to disengage and feel relaxed.

Step 1: Place both hands on your lower belly (the space below your navel). Position them palm on top of palm.

Step 2: Close your eyes and visualize a small, golden flower beneath your hands. Feel the gentle warmth it radiates.

Step 3: Take a long, slow breath in. As you exhale, imagine the flower growing bigger and brighter. Feel the heat increase as it gently blooms.

Step 4: Continue to focus on the warmth and your breath. Imagine the flower traveling up through your body, filling your stomach and chest with soothing energy. Feel it glide up your throat, into your head, and into the space behind your eyes. Breathe in the light and let the calmness settle within.

Step 5: Finally, imagine that the flower passes through the top of your head, where it fully opens and extends its petals, bathing you in a golden glow of positive energy.

get summer ready

At this time of year, we expose more of ourselves to the world. We spend lots of time outdoors with friends and family, and we're also likely to shed the layers if the sun is shining. This makes summer the perfect season to say "yes" to who you are, and fully accept yourself.

For some, the summer can be a difficult time. Being so open and "out there" can make us feel vulnerable and self-conscious. We have a tendency to put the good stuff to the back of our minds and focus on all the things we've done wrong. To restore balance and help you feel loved, set some time aside to *"appreciate my inner beauty and feel at peace with who I am."* This mantra will help boost self-esteem, which in turn makes you feel more relaxed and composed. When you learn to do this, you feel a greater sense of peace because you're comfortable in your own skin.

this week CREATE A COMPLIMENT JAR

How many compliments do you receive? You probably find this question hard to answer because you brush them off or forget them. Set some time aside each evening this week to make a compliment jar that will restore the balance—remember all the things you can do and celebrate all the wonderful things about you. Keep adding to the jar every day. Choose a compliment every time you need a pick-me-up, or as a reminder to value yourself.

Monday: Collect together the items you will need: a large, empty jar, a sticky label or sticky note, and a pen and some paper. On the label or sticky note write "Compliments Jar" and stick it somewhere on the lid.

Tuesday: What personal compliments have you been paid? Even if you can't remember specific comments, spend today thinking about your friends and family and all the things they appreciate about you, or say that you do well.

Wednesday: Spend some time reflecting on your day. There will be moments that you have excelled—perhaps you helped someone, or went above and beyond to achieve a goal. Every success counts.

Thursday: Are there any moments of kindness in your life that nobody else knows about? Write them down and pop them in the jar.

Friday: Write down all of the things that you think you do well on separate pieces of paper. Don't be shy about this. It's your time to shine and revel in your achievements and all the good things that make you, you! Pop them inside the jar.

At the weekend: When you have some time this weekend, read through the different compliments. Bask in the glow and take a moment to appreciate yourself.

this weekend ACCEPT YOURSELF

You might be tempted to rush this exercise, particularly if you're not comfortable with your appearance, but try to take your time. You can begin this weekend and then practice throughout the week too. Make a point of repeating this exercise often and you will see and feel the benefits, as you become more self-assured and at peace with yourself.

Step 1: Stand in front of a full-length mirror. If you haven't got one, use a large mirror where you can at least see the top half of your body and your face.

Step 2: Gaze at your reflection lovingly. Instead of focusing on any perceived imperfections, look at yourself as a whole—as the person who lives your life and is the center of your world. Say *"I love you"* and mean it. If it feels awkward, that's fine. Keep repeating this phrase and there will come a moment when it doesn't feel as strange.

Step 3: Smile and look at how your face lights up. Stand tall and lengthen your spine. Notice how this makes you look and feel more confident. See the twinkle in your eyes and the curve of your lips. Acknowledge your inner and outer beauty.

Step 4: Thank your body for carrying you this far and appreciate all that it does for you each day.

a sunny smile

A sunny day makes you feel good. It puts a spring in your step and a smile on your face. Even if the weather is under par, you can still bring the essence of summer to life and instill a sense of calm contentment in everything you do by wearing a smile.

It might sound tricky, particularly if you're lacking energy or feeling stressed, but that's the time you should be smiling! This facial expression takes fewer muscles than a frown, so you'll be expending less energy, and it also has the power to change your mood. The physical act of a smile stimulates your emotions and encourages them to follow suit.

smile at the world

Check in with your smile at any point during the day. Take a deep breath and imagine that you are drawing soothing energy up through your body to your face. Smile, and as you do so, remember *"my smile radiates warmth and joy!"* The more you smile, the more people smile back at you, which also helps you feel the love.

the powerful sun

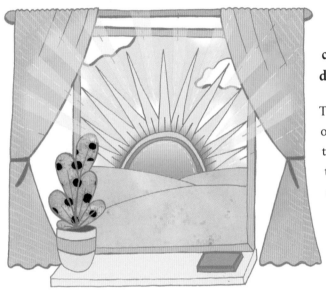

The sun was, and still is, a symbol of harmony and warmth and a comforting presence, particularly during the summer months.

Throughout history the sun has been a source of fascination. The Ancients delighted in telling tales to explain its existence and how it rises through the sky, from glistening chariots carrying fiery sun gods and goddesses, to an ever-present ball of light that could be harnessed in many ways.

To those early civilizations, the sun was all-consuming, and they must have spent a fair amount of time beneath its golden rays. No wonder they embraced its power. The benefits of all that sunshine would have been more energy, better sleep, a stronger, fitter body, and a joyful mood. You can follow suit by celebrating the sun and tapping into its energy.

feel empowered

Keep the soothing energy of the sun in your heart every day by greeting this fiery orb as you would an old friend. Get out of bed and place your feet firmly on the floor. Draw a long breath in. Elongate your spine and feel the stretch. Move to the window and throw back the drapes or blinds. Do this with flair and excitement—remember, this is the start of a new day, and the sun has chosen to shine on you! Even if it isn't a sunny day, there is still light inside you, so embrace it. Stand for a moment and look out at the world. Feel the presence of the sun casting its gentle warmth upon you. Imagine that you are standing in its glare, soaking in those powerful, loving rays.

visualization A BALL OF GOLDEN LIGHT

Tap into the soothing energy of the sun with a beautiful meditation. This meditation can be done inside or out, depending on how you feel, but if you do venture outdoors, remember to apply the sunscreen.

Step 1: Find somewhere comfortable to sit where you won't be disturbed. To begin, close your eyes, relax your body, and take a few deep breaths to center yourself.

Step 2: Imagine there's a tiny ball of golden light sitting in the middle of your chest. As you breathe it gets bigger and brighter, so for every inhalation the ball expands, spreading its light outward. Soon, the light becomes all-encompassing and shines from every pore, surrounding you in a vibrant halo.

Step 3: As you continue to breathe, turn up the brightness even more so that you become the glowing ball of fire. Feel the warmth permeate your being, feel it spread to every part of your body, soothe all your aches and pains, and chase away any fear that you have.

Step 4: Now imagine that, like the rising sun, you are lifting upward into the sky. You are as light as a feather and floating among the clouds. Relax and enjoy this moment of peace. Let the light envelop you in gentle warmth. Rest here and revel in the glow of your vibrance.

Step 5: When you are ready, gradually return to earth and bring the light into your chest once more. Focus on the tiny golden sun sitting at your heart and know that it is always present to soothe and calm you.

savor the season

Summer is about taking time out, and taking your time. The heat demands that you slow down and uncoil, like a snake languishing in the shade. Taking the time to nourish your body with rest, plenty of water, and good food is essential during the summer months.

We know the benefits of drinking plenty of water, especially on a hot, sunny day. Staying hydrated helps you to deal with stress more effectively, clear the mind, and maintain energy levels, all of which give you a greater sense of peace.

Summer ingredients, too, should be enjoyed at this time of year—making the most of fresh, seasonal food is extremely good for mind, body, and soul. Food is also the perfect excuse to get together with family and reconnect with friends, to plan lots of exciting fun experiences, and to relax. An al fresco picnic (see opposite) is the perfect way to do this, particularly if you make it a mindful event.

foods that hydrate

Your water intake can be boosted by the foods you eat, and the benefits of this are twofold. Not only will you be hydrated, you'll also be taking in important nutrients and vitamins.

Take a snack pack of seasonal fresh fruit like strawberries, peaches, raspberries, melon, and cherries to work with you, so that you're fully hydrated throughout the day. Consider this an instant calm fix and nibble when you need a moment's respite.

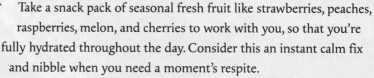

sensory A SUMMER PICNIC

This the season to make the most of the weather, to get outside and enjoy the sunshine, the long, lazy days, and warm, vibrant evenings. Being mindful means engaging with all of your senses and experiencing each moment fully. So, during your picnic, try to remain aware of what is going on around you.

Step 1: As you lay your picnic blanket down on the ground, feel the softness against your skin and how the earth feels underfoot. You might feel the dampness of the grass beneath your fingers.

Step 2: Notice any fragrance in the air and how the sun warms your skin. Take in your surroundings. What can you see and hear? From the chatter of your nearest and dearest to those farther afield, like children playing in the distance, a dog barking, or the sound of bees buzzing around the flowers. Pick up on each thread of sound.

Step 3: As you take your first bite of a sandwich or sip of drink, notice how it feels in your mouth. Consider the texture and taste. Take your time chewing and savoring each mouthful. How does it feel to be eating outside? Does it add to the joy? Notice the expressions of others and how they feel.

Step 4: As you share food and conversation, really make those connections and listen with intent as you converse. Remember, there is no need to rush anything—this picnic is about slowing down and enjoying each moment.

MANTRA FOR THE WEEK:

*"I savor the taste of the season,
as I savor each moment."*

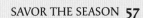

go with the flow

Summer is the perfect time to embrace spontaneity. It's the sunshine season when anything goes—so seize the day!

The plants and flowers dance beneath the light of the fiery orb, while the butterflies find their true colors. Busy bees are drawn to the prettiest blooms and the animals and birds flit and frolic to their heart's content. The days are longer and the nights brighter, providing a world of opportunity for all. Take inspiration from your surroundings and learn to go with the flow, wherever that may be.

You might not associate spontaneity with finding inner peace but the two are connected. When you act on instinct, you are following your intuition and responding to the call within, that says: *"I am centered and open to the flow."* You are allowing yourself the freedom to be who you are, to do what you want, and to live in the moment. All of these things contribute to how you feel and create a sense of serenity within.

Some people find it hard to let go and be spontaneous. There is an element of risk involved, but once you get over the fear of going with the flow, you'll discover there is joy to be found in seizing the moment.

this week BE SPONTANEOUS

This week, attempt to be more spontaneous in your attitude and approach to life by reflecting on how you think, feel, and act in your journal. Each day, use these suggestions as prompts to help you explore a more spontaneous mindset.

Monday: Today, take special care to tune into your instincts and recognize how you feel in each moment. For example, if you get a tingle of excitement in your stomach when you think about doing something, go with it. Accept that your intuition is driving you forward.

Tuesday: Spend some time today reflecting on the past. Bring to mind a time when you were spontaneous. Perhaps you said "yes" to something you wouldn't normally do—how did this feel and what was the outcome? Relive the emotions and recognize that it's okay to act on impulse.

Wednesday: What would happen if you gave yourself a completely free day? Imagine that you did not have to do any of the things you might normally do. What does an empty diary feel like? What emotions rise to the surface? Are you excited? Nervous? Anxious? Then consider why you feel this way, and if you could change that mindset.

Thursday: Do you know anyone who lives spontaneously? Perhaps there's a person you admire who tends to go with the flow. What could you learn from them and how can you harness these qualities yourself?

Friday: Think about some of the things you have discovered about yourself this week. What would allow you to be more spontaneous? In your journal, list some ways in which you could do this. For example, doing some work on your self-esteem or learning a new skill.

At the weekend: Take action! If there is an activity you feel like doing this weekend, just go ahead and do it!

shake it up

Inner peace comes in many forms, but it is often found when we stretch ourselves and do something that challenges us. When you step outside your comfort zone and try something new, the experience lifts you and boosts your confidence.

When you feel energized, you feel ready for anything. It has a knock-on effect on your mindset and the way you feel about the world around you. You're less likely to let fear take over, which puts you in a place of peace and power. You'll feel a sense of renewal, which is life-affirming. The good news is, you don't have to do anything extreme. Small steps in a new direction are enough to improve your well-being and create a sense of harmony.

step outside your comfort zone

Do something out of the ordinary. A few small, simple changes every day can make a huge difference to how you feel inside. Here are some ideas to get you started:

- If you have a usual coffee place that you always visit, try somewhere new.

- Divert from your normal commute to work or running route and choose a different path or location.

- Get up early for a walk, rather than venture out in the car later.

- Say hello to someone new or start up a conversation in the grocery store.

- Try cooking a completely new recipe.

- If you normally go out as a family to the local park, go farther afield and try somewhere different, or visit a nature reserve.

rest and restore

Most hot countries have an afternoon siesta. Everything stops for nap time, as it's considered an important part of the day. It's essential to rest, especially when the weather is hot, which makes summer the ideal season to recharge.

While you might feel that it's just an excuse to be lazy, an afternoon snooze is the perfect way to disconnect from the world and offload any mind clutter. A few precious moments of peace, when you either sit or lay in silence and disengage from everything that is going on around you, will imbue you with tranquility, improve your mental agility, and provide a quick energy boost.

Why not go a step further and take some time out to meditate (see the Beach Paradise meditation on page 62)? A meditation is the perfect way to relax at any point during the week or weekend. Treat it as a luxury and really enjoy the experience by telling yourself: *"I listen to my body, and ensure it is rested and cared for."* You can do this outside in the backyard if you want to make the most of the weather, or first thing in the morning, or even before bed.

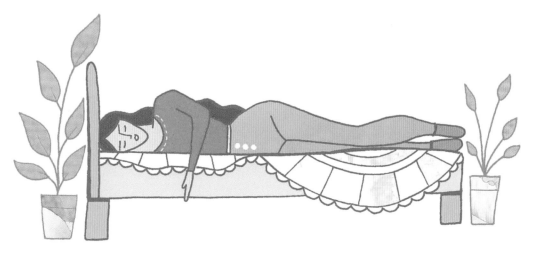

this weekend HAVE A SIESTA

Allow yourself 40 minutes to completely disconnect from the world. Even if you don't nod off, the rest time will help you recharge and calm your mind.

You might want to snooze outside and let the sounds of nature help you drift off. Otherwise, lay on top of your bed or the sofa, or just sit in a comfy chair, but make sure to have plenty of support, soft cushions, and blankets so that you feel nurtured. If it helps, light a scented candle to create a soothing atmosphere.

visualization BEACH PARADISE

Make a point of practicing this meditation a few times over the week ahead and notice how it makes you feel.

Step 1: Gather everything you need to be comfortable, such as a mat and a cushion. Make sure you won't be disturbed. Turn your phone off so that you can completely disconnect from the world. Lay down on the mat with your head supported by the cushion.

Step 2: Close your eyes and inhale deeply. As you release the breath slowly, push your spine gradually into the mat, taking each vertebra at a time so that you can feel the connection with the earth. Continue to breathe deeply and relax your body.

Step 3: Imagine you are laying on a secluded beach. You can feel the sand beneath you, supporting your weight. It cushions you in comfort. You can see the beautiful blue sky above your head. It is filled with soft, fluffy, white clouds, which stream lazily past. You can hear the gentle ebb and flow of the waves as they lap at the shore. In the distance you can hear a gull calling—a solitary cry, which reminds you that you are alone upon this glorious stretch of beach.

Step 1: Set a timer, close your eyes, and settle into a restful position. Focus on your breathing and the rise and fall of your chest.

Step 2: If worries cloud your mind, try not to focus on them. Instead, let them flow out of your head. Continue to concentrate on the rhythm of your breathing. Let your muscles relax into the soft surface of the bed or cushions and let yourself go.

Step 3: Once the timer sounds, give yourself a couple of minutes to acclimatize. Stretch your limbs and give them a gentle shake to get your circulation moving and boost energy.

Step 4: You breathe in, and you notice a faint citrus scent mingling with the saltiness of the sea. You breathe out and feel the warmth of the sun envelope your body. You are completely at peace in this moment. Every part of your body is relaxed. You revel in the stillness. Breathe in, breathe out, and let go of any stress you have been holding on to.

Step 5: Linger in this beach paradise for as long as you want. This is your opportunity to completely relax. When you are ready, bring your attention back to your breathing and feel your body pressing into the floor. Open your eyes and give your limbs a shake.

Next Steps: Once you are familiar with the narrative of this meditation and have practiced it a few times, have a go at changing something. For example, you might want to go for a stroll along the shoreline and dip your feet into the cooling water, or you could imagine that you are floating on the surface of the sea, with the beach in the distance. This is your meditation and you have creative control, so use your imagination and enjoy!

the sounds of summer

There's one sound of nature that is associated with the summer months. It's the soothing hum of bees at work, flitting from flower to flower and taking their fill of pollen and nectar.

Sound has the power to calm your mind and invoke peace. Whether you are listening to the bees (see opposite) or your own musical selection, acknowledge that *"the sounds of nature soothe my soul."*

this weekend SING A LULLABY

It's during your day-to-day activities that you're most likely to seek a moment of tranquility. Be prepared and keep your favorite tune to hand, to calm your mind when you're busy with tasks.

In the morning, pick a song or a melody that instantly puts you at ease. Play it a couple of times as you get ready for your day, and then rewind and repeat in your head throughout the day.

Each time you play the song in your mind, breathe deeply and engage with the tune. Feel the music imbue you with a sense of peace. Close your eyes for a couple of seconds and imagine you're wrapped from head to toe in white satin. Hold that image in your mind. Even if you can't recall all of the melody, repeat what you know and let it fill with you soothing energy.

sensory A GENTLE HUM

Let the bees help you unwind. Their gentle buzz is deep, melodic, and almost hypnotic, and can calm a busy mind, helping you to relax. It is a background noise that also makes the perfect accompaniment to any meditation.

Step 1: Sit in a comfy chair or on the ground by a flowering plant. Lavender and lilac are both favorites of the bees, so if you have those in the backyard, set yourself up nearby. You'll also benefit from the lovely aroma that they emit.

Step 2: Close your eyes and focus on the gentle thrum of the bee's humming. Notice the level and tone of the noise and follow each strand of sound. Let this soothing noise surround you as you breathe deeply. Let it fill your mind and clear away any worry or fear.

Step 3: Place your hands on your upper chest (just below your throat). Take a long, deep breath and make a low "mmmm" sound. You should feel the gentle vibration within your chest and also beneath your palms.

Step 4: Continue to make the noise, releasing the sound with each inhalation. Imagine that as you let go of the breath and produce the note, you are releasing any tension from your body.

Step 5: To finish, bring your attention back to the song of the bees. Relax, recline, and enjoy their sweet music.

reconnect with nature

As the weather heats up, we leave our homes and venture outside. The landscape is lifted by the light and warmth, as we are too.

Exposed to the sunshine and exploring our surroundings, we feel more confident, upbeat, and connected to the natural world. Harnessing the power of nature is a little like plugging into an energy source—you instantly feel the difference. The benefits are numerous, from feeling more alive, energized, and optimistic, to being soothed and inspired by what you see and feel.

seek out sunflowers

Sunflowers are synonymous with the summer months. These gorgeous blooms capture the essence of the season in the way they look, and also the way they follow the sun's path through the sky. They have a vibrant "look-at-me" beauty that stands out from the crowd. Even if you're not a fan, you'll be able to appreciate the joy and brightness they bring.

Take a moment out of your busy schedule to admire the joyful bloom of sunflowers and you will feel the benefits. If you have them in your backyard, take some time to stand with them and watch how they react to the sun's light. Imagine you're a sunflower bathed in golden rays, as you stand tall and centered.

Alternatively, treat yourself to a bunch of sunflowers and position them in a vase in your window. Sit and gaze at the flower heads. Notice their size, shape, and structure. Breathe in the beauty of the blooms and let them infuse you with positive, peaceful energy.

"My connection with nature refreshes and renews my spirit."

be a stargazer

Looking up at the night sky is a magical experience at any time, but particularly on a clear night during the summer months. It allows you a moment of stillness when you can be present and witness the glory of the universe above your head.

Treat yourself to a fragment of peace at the end of each day by sitting, standing, or even laying beneath the night sky. You don't have to do anything else except let your gentle gaze take in the vista before you.

Breathe, and imagine that the sky is a soft blanket, an ever-present layer of comfort that you can tap into. Look at the pretty patterns of the stars and see the constellations form before your eyes. Even if you can't make out the map of the skies, simply enjoy what you can see. Let your mind drift upward and offload the stress of the day in this moment of serenity.

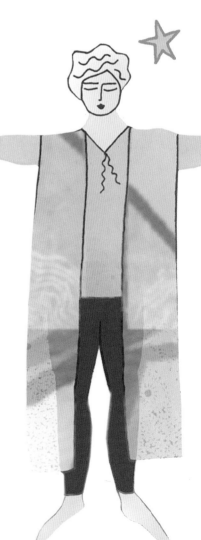

caress the earth

The earth is alive. It bristles with energy throughout the year. It has a rhythm that you can tune into at any time to feel anchored and safe, to center yourself, and re-establish your connection with the natural world. In doing so, you will be able to recharge and find the stillness you seek.

Working with the land and doing your bit for the environment helps to cement your relationship with nature. By taking the time to care, you are investing something of yourself in the world around you. Doing something for the environment creates a strong link with your natural roots. You feel good, and the earth feels even better.

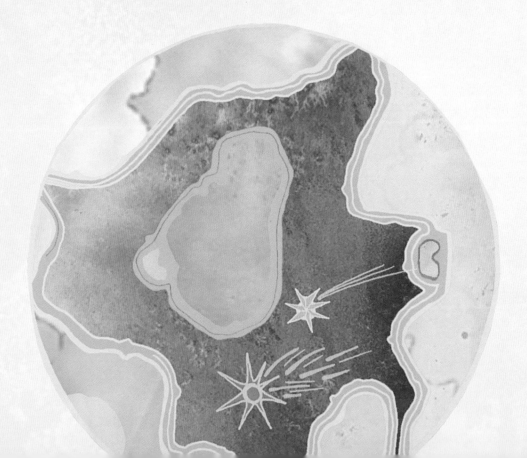

this week A HELPING HAND

The time you have available may vary, but if you make the effort this week to spend some time outdoors and give something back to nature, you will feel the benefits.

Monday: Find a piece of nature—a plot of land, the local park or community gardens, or even in the street outside your house—and go litter picking.

Tuesday: Tend to your own backyard, from deadheading flowers to clearing space for them to breathe by pulling out the weeds. Anything you can do to give nature a helping hand will re-establish your connection with the earth. If you don't have a backyard, why not offer to help an elderly neighbor out by cutting the grass?

Wednesday: Volunteer with your local wildlife group. From restoring hedges and stone walls to clearing rubbish from rivers and streams, there are plenty of jobs that need doing to help the environment in your area.

Thursday: Do your bit for wildlife by feeding the birds and cleaning out any existing feeders. Put water out, too, or a little birdbath, so they can cool down in the heat.

Friday: Put up a bee box or create an insect hotel by recycling bits of wood, tubes, and piping. Look for inspiration on the internet or buy a brand-new one and install it somewhere in your backyard.

At the weekend: Take the time to appreciate your efforts this weekend. Sit outside, look at the changes you have made, and notice how nature is already responding. Perhaps there are more pollinators around the flowers or bugs in your insect hotel? Enjoy the peaceful environment you have created.

stay cool and calm

Work with the element of water to help cool turbulent emotions, soothe body and mind, and embrace the flow of love in your life.

This season, work on opening your heart, so that you increase the amount of love you give and receive. This in turn will have an effect on your peace of mind. One of the quickest ways to avoid discord and feel instantly calm—especially when everyone around you is feeling the heat—is to turn your temperature down. This isn't always easy to do at the height of summer, but you can use the element of water to help you feel at peace with the world around you.

turn it down

If you have access to a bathroom, you can carry out this ritual with a mini visualization once a day. Even if you're feeling calm, it provides a moment to switch off and embrace cooling energy.

Stand at the sink and switch on the cold tap to medium flow. Position both wrists in the flow. Close your eyes and feel the icy coolness travel along each arm, over your shoulders, and into your chest. It helps if you can visualize bright, white energy sweeping through your body. Bring your attention to the space behind your eyes, and feel the cool energy settle there. Take a couple of deep breaths and really embrace the iciness of the water. Say **"My energy is fluid; I move through the world with ease and calm."** Then open your eyes and remove your wrists from the flow.

this weekend DIP YOUR FEET IN THE WATER

There's nothing like a paddle in the sea. It's refreshing, restorative, and a lovely way to enjoy the sunshine. If you can't get to the coast, then a river or stream can provide the same benefits on your doorstep. Even if you're not a fan of getting your feet wet, simply sitting by free-flowing water (like a fountain) will help you feel relaxed. Try these tips for yourself and let a wave of inner peace take over mind and body.

Step 1: Revel in the stillness and fix your gaze upon the flow of the water. Simply breathe in and out as you follow the direction of the ripples.

Step 2: If there is anything on your mind, imagine throwing it into the water and watch as it drifts away from you. To help with this visualization, use a pebble, stone, or shell. Bring it up to your lips and let your outward breath infuse it with any stress you are carrying, then toss it into the water.

Step 3: Pay attention to what you see and feel in the moment. Check in with yourself, to make sure you are not holding any tension in your body.

Step 4: Stand for a while and let the water move over your toes. Notice how it feels as it gently cleanses each foot. Use this moment to set an intention for peace. You might simply say in your head, or out loud if you feel comfortable doing so, *"I carry calmness at my heart."*

visualization MELT YOUR HEART

Lavender is the quintessential summer plant with its calming aroma and vibrant color. Combined with the soothing properties of water this is a powerful herb for inner peace. Find out how to reap the benefits.

Step 1: Collect together an ice-cube mold and some lavender essential oil. Fill the molds halfway with water, add a couple of drops of the essential oil, then top up the molds with water. Pop in the freezer. You might want to label the cubes so that you know they're not to be used in drinks.

Step 2: When the ice cubes have formed, remove one or two cubes from the molds and wrap in a handkerchief or a piece of muslin (cheesecloth). Sit or lay outside in the sun. Place the ice parcel you have created on your forehead for a minute. Close your eyes and enjoy the cooling sensation against your skin. Breathe deeply and let your mind clear of any worry.

Step 3: Place the parcel in the middle of your chest, over your Heart chakra, the energy center associated with your emotions. Leave the parcel there, for the ice to gradually melt. Continue to breathe deeply and let your mind drift as your Heart chakra gently opens. Inhale the aroma of the lavender as the ice melts, and relax.

letting go

You have already discovered the beauty of a sunrise, and how witnessing the dawn of a new day can help you feel centered and ready for anything (see page 48). The same can be said for a sunset. It is a poignant and peaceful moment when you can let the stress of the day slip from your shoulders and appreciate the wonder of nature.

As the long summer evenings linger into autumn, set some time aside to enjoy the experience. You don't need anything else except an open heart and mind to appreciate what you see.

catch a sunset

Choose a location that is easy to get to, and where you are sure to have a good view of the sun as it sets. For most people, a chair in the front or backyard is the ideal setting. If you're feeling particularly artistic you might want to keep a journal and a pen with you.

Sit and wait in the stillness. Don't force yourself to think about anything—this is an opportunity to switch off from the world and enjoy some serenity. Gaze at the view, at the sky as it slowly changes color before your eyes, and notice any shift in atmosphere. You might sense the gentle transition into nighttime, the sounds of nature slowly retreating, and a heaviness in the air.

Breathe in the beauty of the moment, and as you exhale, feel any tension leaving your body. Relax and embrace the peace.

chapter 3

AUTUMN

a blaze of autumn

As the wheel of the year turns once more, moving into autumn doesn't mean that all the light has gone. Summer's hazy glow often lingers, stretching spectral fingers over the colorful landscape. Reluctant to leave the earth completely, she adds a burnished brightness to the cooling days.

Autumn is not a harsh transition, but an aging of sorts, and a kind way for us to become acclimatized to the changes. The ecosystem slowly withdraws into itself and Mother Nature urges us to do the same, to take some time out to evaluate how far we have come and where we are heading next.

Peace in this environment is easily found in quiet moments snuggled beneath layers of fleecy blankets, or the stillness of a fresh autumn morning, as the mist slowly rises like the steam from a freshly poured mug of coffee. It is even discovered in a blast of breeze that whips at hair and pinches at cheeks—it is those "slap-in-the-face" reminders that tell us we are alive, we are vital, and we count. Peace isn't always about being quiet. While it thrives in tranquility and chills in the heat of the midday sun, it can also exist in the harshest of

> *"I saw old autumn in the misty morn
> stand shadowless like silence,
> listening to silence."*

Thomas Hood

environments, where it represents balance amid change, and the ability
to go with the flow and release negative energy.

letting go with the last of the leaves

After the full-throttle vibrance of summer, it can be a challenge to retreat
and settle into the longer, darker days. You may want to hold on to the
sunshine thrills a little longer, to make the days last into the nights, and
keep the vacation dream going. But the more you try to resist, the harder
it becomes to find the calmness within because you are going against
the grain of time. Some changes need to be embraced wholeheartedly.
Each season should be viewed as a new chapter in the story of your
life, and like any good work of fiction, it will have its highs and lows,
which in truth, are one and the same thing.

Autumn is about slowing down, which naturally lends itself to stillness. It is about setting yourself a new steadier pace, accepting that it's time to take your foot off the gas, and releasing the pressure. You have come so far and you should acknowledge each hard-won success. Consider this the harvest season, the perfect time to examine what you have achieved and to give thanks for each gift. In doing so, you will not only feel a rich sense of satisfaction and joy, but you will also see opportunities for growth in the future. It is the time to let go of fear and guilt and to release the things that no longer serve you, which in turn will help you discover a deeper sense of tranquility. Blow away the cobwebs—literally—and you'll feel renewed to your core and at peace with the world around you. Most importantly, do not be afraid to get out and about. While the days may be colder and darker, they are still filled with glorious color, which has the power to make your heart sing and put some zing in your step.

embrace the elements

In this section you will find suggestions to help you foster inner peace, including working with the changes in the environment and embracing the elements, from quick-fix stress busters to more in-depth exercises and

rituals that you can enjoy at your leisure. You will discover how to harness the power of the darker evenings, restore balance, and boost creativity. You will understand the importance of letting go and accepting things as they are, for what they are. You will see the beauty in your inner and outer landscape, and you will recognize the value you continue to bring to the world by reflecting upon past victories and planning for the future. You will learn to listen to yourself, to your body and mind, and to the prompts and calls from nature's songbook. All these things work together to help you find a deep well of serenity, which will carry you through any turbulence and help you emerge into the light—composed, confident, and with a renewed sense of calm.

AUTUMN WATCH

If you only do one thing this autumn, take the time to focus on what you have achieved so far. Revel in your successes and learn from the things that didn't work out. Recognize how far you have come and be thankful for all the blessings in your life. Autumn is the time to reap the rewards of everything you have put in motion, so enjoy the harvest of your hard work and celebrate being you!

brace yourself

Biting autumn wind may take your breath away, but think of it as a gift from nature and an easy way to de-stress at any point during the day.

Set some time aside this week to fully appreciate the fluctuations in the weather. By honoring this shift and the seasonal cycles, you'll appreciate the fluctuations you experience in your own mood and energy levels.

blow away your worries

Whether you're at work, at home, or nipping to the store, you can take a minute every day to stand still and feel the air moving around you. Wrap up warm and slip outside. Close your eyes and focus on how the breeze buffets your skin.

Take a long, deep breath in, and as you exhale, let the wind carry your worries away. Imagine any anxiety and residual negative energy leaving your body with your outward breath. Take at least three cleansing breaths like this. Feel a sense of calmness settle within, as the wind wraps its blustery arms around you.

MANTRA FOR THE WEEK:

"I am grateful for change and the gift that it brings."

sensory A BLUSTERY WALK

The key to this walk is to take your time. The length of the walk matters less than what you put into it. This is not a brisk walk; it's a meander through nature. Experience the walk fully through each sense and you'll feel a sense of wonder growing at the beauty of the world around you.

Step 1: Before you leave, wrap up and wear suitable footwear.

Step 2: Choose a location to walk and experience the elements, somewhere like a local park, the countryside, or even your own backyard. As you stroll, engage all your senses.

Step 3: Think about what you can see. Notice any changes, like the color and consistency of the leaves. Draw in the view, as if you were gazing at a landscape portrait, and connect with the vibrant hues of the season.

Step 4: Listen. Pay attention to the sounds of nature: the rustle of tiny creatures in the undergrowth and the sound of dried leaves crunching beneath your feet.

Step 5: Engage your sense of smell and notice the musky aroma of the earth. Breathe deeply and let the taste of the air touch your tongue.

Step 6: Reach out and touch the bark of the trees, then gather a handful of leaves and let them fall through your fingers. Press each foot deep into the ground as you walk.

Step 7: Stop for a moment and check in with yourself. How do you feel right now? Recharged? At peace? Relaxed?

Step 8: As you continue your walk, look for a memento that you can keep, to remind you of this feeling. Something small that you can easily carry, like a pine cone, acorn, pretty stone, or colorful leaf, is perfect. When you get home, place the memento somewhere you can see it and be reminded of the sense of wonder you experienced.

be still

This time of year, everything slows down. It feels as if nature has hit the pause button. It's time to go within, to reflect on and evaluate what has gone before.

Daily chores and responsibilities can get in the way of this sense of winding down, so it's important to build time for yourself into your schedule. Try to remember that **"stillness is my sanctuary."** Once you have acclimatized to having quiet time, when you do absolutely nothing but sit with yourself, it will, over time, help to calm your mind and bring about a sense of peace.

do nothing

Instead of trying to cram in five minutes here and there, block out some time in your calendar. Give yourself ten minutes each day throughout the week to sit and do nothing. If you find it hard to do this in the day, do it just before bed. Switch everything off, including your phone, and be completely still. Focus on the rise and fall of your chest, and nothing else. If your mind wanders and you find yourself fretting, just bring your attention back to your breathing. Let the silence envelope you and relax. Make this a regular practice, and you will soon be able to recreate this meditation quickly, whenever you need a moment of respite.

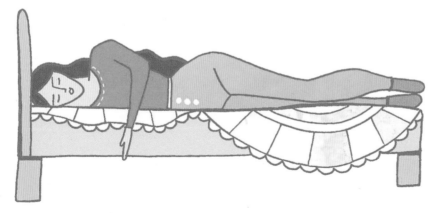

visualization SILENCE IS GOLDEN

Challenge yourself to an hour of silence as you practice this simple breathing technique. Take the time to practice so that you can call on it whenever you feel stressed. This technique should provide the comfort you need to center yourself. Create a soothing atmosphere by burning some calming lavender or relaxing ylang ylang essential oil.

Step 1: To begin, stand with your feet hip-width apart. Alternatively sit, either on the floor with your back against the wall, or in a firm chair with your bottom toward the back. Let your weight fall backward, so that the wall or chair supports you.

Step 2: Roll your shoulders back and lengthen your spine. This helps to open your chest and allows your Heart chakra, the energy center associated with the emotions, to be fully activated. Place both hands upon your chest, right in the center where your Heart chakra is located.

Step 3: Close your eyes and take a couple of long, deep breaths to calm your mind. As you breathe, notice the warmth that spreads from your hands, and how it is absorbed into your chest. You should feel the area soften beneath the heat.

Step 4: Take a deep breath in, and as you exhale, let any emotions that you feel flow through your fingers. Let the gentle warmth soothe these feelings, but don't try and restrict them. You are allowed to feel what you feel.

Step 5: Continue to breathe deeply and feel the heat spread until it fills your chest and stomach. Feel the rise and fall of your diaphragm beneath your fingers and focus on this.

Step 6: When you're ready, slowly open your eyes and relax your body. Breathe deeply and check in with every part, from your head and shoulders, along your spine, and into your legs and feet. Give your body a gentle shake to get things moving again.

create a sanctuary

Your home may be a place where you feel safe, but it can also be a hub of activity. It's important to claim some space for yourself when and where you can.

Just as our home can become cluttered and overwhelming, there are moments in every day when your mind will feel cluttered, too. Your brain is a receptor picking up hundreds of pieces of information at any one time. If you add

this weekend MAKE A SACRED SPACE

A special space or area where you can retreat and be alone with your thoughts will help you feel centered and at peace. Create a space that you can turn into a sacred haven.

Monday: Identify an area in your home where you can claim some space for yourself. This might be a spare room that you can use, or an office space that you can adapt—even a corner of your living room will suffice.

Tuesday: Mark out your area. If you don't want to change anything permanently, then think about items of furniture that you can move and arrange to create a circular space where the healing energy can flow. For example, if you've chosen an area within your living room, you might want to outline this with a circular rug.

Wednesday: Today, consider what you need to create the right ambience for you. Position comfy blankets in the space so that you can sit and snuggle. Collect a few scented candles or an oil burner and select an essential oil to match your needs. For example, lavender will soothe your mind, geranium balances the emotions, while rosemary is vibrant and uplifting. A crystal,

all the thoughts that you have, then it's easy to see how overwhelm happens. It's important to create space in our minds as well as our homes.

In ancient times, healers would often create a sacred space where they could retreat and recharge (see below). You are going to do the same. With a little flexibility, you can change any room in your home to your suit your needs and create a cozy sanctuary away from the world.

like a piece of quartz or rose quartz, is also a good addition, as this will generate positive healing energy. You might want to position the crystal on a coffee table for easy reach, or sit with it in the space you have created.

Thursday: Spend some time today getting used to your new space. Think about how you would like to spend time in your sanctuary and make a list of the things you would like to do when you have some time to yourself.

Friday: Spend five minutes in this space to check in with yourself. Ask, how do I feel right now? Let any thoughts arise. Consider both physical feelings and emotional ones. Acknowledge how you feel and say *"Its okay to feel how I feel."*

At the weekend: Find a comfy spot within the space you have created. If you have crystals, you might want to arrange them either in a circle around you or in front of you. Place the palms of your hands on the floor. Draw a long, deep breath in, and as you exhale, imagine a dome of light forming over you and your sacred space. Continue to breathe and reinforce this image. Know that in this space you are protected. The dome of light shields you from negative energy and recharges your spirit with light and love.

visualization CLEAR YOUR MIND

To restore peace, try this easy visualization. Take a minute to picture this in your mind.

Step 1: Imagine for a moment that your head is a room. See it as a space filled with boxes of different sizes. Picture them heaped high, filling every available space. Each box contains a thought or worry that you don't need.

Step 2: As you breathe, see a chute forming. It appears like a hole in the wall and it's a way of getting rid of all the rubbish you have collected. One by one, pick up each box and throw it down the chute. You can do this as quickly as you like.

Step 3: When you have finished, the room should be completely empty, and you will see a large window at one end. Imagine opening the window and letting all the light and air flow in. Breathe and relax.

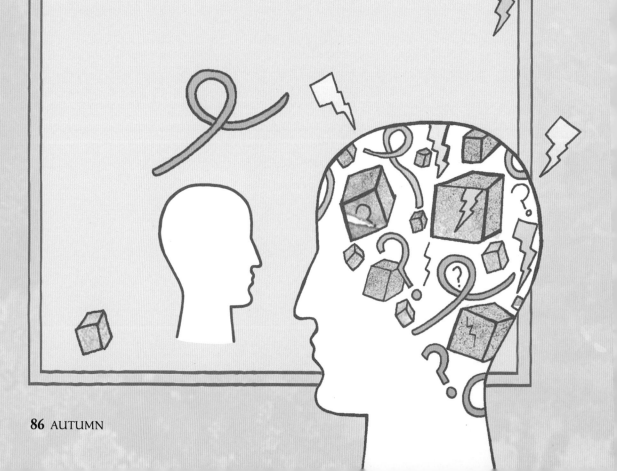

fall

"The Fall" is the perfect way to describe this season as we surrender to the winter months and slip gracefully into transition.

This is not a sudden change; it's a gentle slowing down of everything. Connect with this energy by slowing down your movements. Resist the urge to rush through your days and train your body and mind to take things at an easier pace. Say to yourself, *"I slow my pace and fall into a peaceful state."* As you begin to train your body and mind to slow down, your emotions should also settle. But feelings can be erratic, and you may still experience stress, anger, and turmoil. Instead of resisting these, it helps if you can learn to go with the flow of what you are feeling. Let it move through you and breathe into it. This should calm surging emotions and help you reach a more peaceful state.

slow down

Choose one activity that you do throughout the day and do it with intent. For example, making a cup of your favorite brew can be an experience to savor. Take your time with each step. Wait for the water to boil and use these minutes to do some deep breathing. Pour the hot water into the mug and focus on stirring slowly. Watch as the liquid swirls, and let this simple motion calm your mind. Place your hands either side of the mug and feel the warmth. See the steam rising and feel the moist heat against your skin. Sip quietly and concentrate on the taste of the liquid and how it feels against your tongue.

conquer inner heights

When things seem insurmountable, our natural inclination is to run and hide, whether that's physically or emotionally. We retreat from the situation, or we spend so much time worrying about it that we end up making a mountain out of a molehill.

Climbing a mountain is not so hard. It doesn't matter what size it is. It can be a gradual incline, a hill, or something more challenging. The physical act of moving forward and up gets the heart pumping and the oxygen flowing, and clears the head. When we reach the top, however high it is, we feel a sense of pride. We can see things differently from this vantage point, and a new vista opens up before us.

visualization CLIMB A MOUNTAIN

Let the physical activity of moving upward spur you onward. What you climb is up to you—you could even choose to climb the stairs, but it does help to get outside and experience the wide-open spaces in nature.

Step 1: Push down with the soles of your feet and feel the earth beneath you. This is not a race. Better to take your time and conserve energy for when you might need it.

Step 2: Position each foot with purpose. Keep your destination in mind as you walk and let this propel you forward. Imagine that every step takes you closer to your goal.

Step 3: With each step, take a deep breath and picture your lungs inflating. Feel the air in your chest, and let it fill your mind too. Every time you exhale, imagine clearing your body and mind of any debris that has gathered.

Step 4: When you reach the top, whether it's a set of stairs, a hill, or a mountain, take a deep breath in. Let the air that you inhale restore you. As you release the breath, take in the view. Relax and enjoy this moment of peace and clarity.

autumn's symphony

Each season plays its own melody, with a rhythm and tone that is unique to the time of year. Let autumn be the season that you pay attention to what your body is telling you.

It's easy to ignore the signs when something is wrong. We might not feel happy, but we push negative thoughts to the back of our mind in an attempt to get on with things. In doing so, these thoughts often surface in other more physical ways, causing tension in the body, including headaches, tummy troubles, and muscle aches. You might be so busy that you haven't noticed, or you can't fully appreciate the background music that nature provides, but this is the ideal time to tune in. The more in harmony you can be with your environment, the happier and more at peace with life you will feel, because you're going with the natural flow of things.

listen to your body

Regularly check in with yourself throughout the day. All you need to do is quickly turn your attention to how you feel. Are you experiencing pain in your body, if so where?

MANTRA FOR THE WEEK:

"I treat my body and mind with kindness and respect."

Focus on each muscle group, from the top of your head down to your feet. Notice the areas that feel tight and tense. Breathe healing energy into them by inhaling deeply and then releasing the breath, while focusing on that area.

recognize your true feelings

It's okay to be sad, frustrated, angry, or upset. These are all valid emotions and we can't be positive, or at peace, all of the time. The problem comes when you try to suppress how you feel throughout the day, or on the flip side, if you become so engrossed with these emotions that they consume your every thought, word, and deed.

Be aware of what is going on in your head. Ask yourself, *"How do I feel right now?"* Don't be afraid of the answer. Acknowledge the emotion and say *"It is okay to feel like this right now."* Breathe deeply and accept that this feeling will pass when it is ready. If you practice self-awareness and get into the habit of acknowledging what you feel without judgment, you will begin to notice the array of emotions that you experience throughout each day, and how they come and go. This will help you feel more balanced.

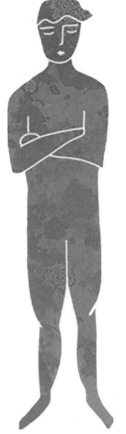

your inner cheerleader

Our body speaks to us in the way that it feels, but our mind also speaks to us, not only in our thoughts but through our inner critic. This is the nagging voice of doubt that you hear daily. Filled with negativity, this voice specializes in picking fault with everything you do. It has the power to make you feel awful if you let it, but the good news is you can swap the inner critic for the inner cheerleader, with a little effort. So pay attention to your thoughts and the way you talk to yourself throughout this week. You will soon start to banish negativity naturally.

sensory WALK IN TUNE WITH NATURE

During your commute to and from work, or when you nip to the store, or walk the dog, let nature dictate your pace. Treat each walk, however small, as an occasion. Seize the chance to experience the symphony of life.

Step 1: Breathe deeply and inhale your surroundings. Do you feel like taking your time, or does the nip in the air make you want to walk faster?

Step 2: Listen to the tap, tap of your feet as they hit the ground. Does it fit with the environment and what you can see and feel?

Step 3: What else can you hear? The roar of the traffic? Car horns? The whoosh of the breeze? Notice how these sounds meld together to create a background rhythm.

autumn's bounty

From colorful fruit and veg to an array of vibrant foliage in the landscape, autumn is a cornucopia of bright hues and tones.

As the days get colder it's natural to crave comfort food. This is a primal instinct going back to those early cave dwellers and hunters, who would have feasted as much as possible in order to store fat for the winter. Unlike them, food is not in short supply for us, but that doesn't mean that we shouldn't follow suit and include some hearty and nutritious meals in our diet.

At home, too, immersing yourself in the shades of the season will help to boost positive energy and promote feelings of peace and abundance. Think of it like enriching your diet, but this time you're introducing elements of nature into your home to lift your mood.

eat seasonally

Look out for seasonal fruit and vegetables that you can include in stews, soups, and smoothies, like squash, pumpkin, celery, cabbage, carrots, apples, and blackberries, and also different types of nuts and seeds.

Every day, make a point of including at least a couple of these things in your daily menu. From a handful of almonds to an apple or a snack pack of carrots, you can enjoy these quick eats on the run.

If you prefer, challenge yourself to try a soup or stew using some of the heartier vegetables. Eating in this way aligns you with the energy of the season, which promotes feelings of well-being.

this week BRING THE OUTSIDE IN

This week, forage for some seasonal items to create a display that will bring the outside in—just make sure to keep a bag or a container with you so you can collect anything that you spot.

Monday: On your daily commute, if you see something colorful that makes you smile, take a closer look. If it's small enough to carry, add it to your bag.

Tuesday: Make an errand more fun. Pay attention to your surroundings as you walk, and let things catch your eye. Make this an adventure and enjoy every moment of your search.

Wednesday: Wrap up warm and visit your backyard, or another outdoor space like a park or nature reserve. Look out for brightly colored leaves and stones, pine cones, conkers, acorns, and other gifts of the season.

Thursday: Lay out your findings and think about how you might like to display them. For example, you could choose a decorative bowl, pop the items inside, and position them in the center of your dinner table. You might want to display them separately in different locations such as on a windowsill, a shelf, or a coffee table. Or you might choose to create a wreath with the autumnal gifts you have collected. A selection of leaves, berries, and twigs can be intertwined with strong yarn or added to a premade wreath to give it an authentic and individual look.

Friday: Spend time making your display. Have fun with this and tune into your inner designer.

At the weekend: When you're done, admire your new décor and how it makes you feel. If you've created a table display, why not invite some friends around for a meal so you can all appreciate the gifts of the season? Or if you have made a wreath, display it in a window or on your door so that everyone can enjoy your efforts.

light the flame

The nights are drawing in and darkness creeps steadily to your door. Before you know it, all the lights are on, filling your home with brightness and relinquishing the shadows. It's only natural to seek the light at this time of year, but the darkness also has its gifts.

In ancient times, the fire was a place where everyone gathered. It was the heart of the home, being the hearth and a place of heat, security, and where all the cooking was carried out. It was also used in rituals to give thanks to the gods and in celebrations, as a focal point. People would gather in a large circle around the fire and tell stories and share their truths. Sometimes they would dance around the flames or throw offerings into the burning embers, as a way of releasing what they no longer needed and making way for something new.

In this autumnal season you, too, can discover that *"the flame within illuminates my world."* Harness the energy of fire to warm your soul, burn away negativity, or simply to light your home with a delightful glow.

burn brightly

Instead of reaching for the light switch, invest in some beautiful candles and position them around your living space. Wait for the darkness to settle and light each one in turn. As you do, imagine that you are igniting a spark within. Feel the warmth in your belly, as the flame begins to flicker and twist. Just as the room is filled with a soft, soothing glow, so you too feel a sense of serenity within, which grows like the flame of each candle.

this week CIRCLE OF FIRE

Autumn is a time of letting go. Create a ring of fire using tealights to banish the shadows and relinquish negative thoughts.

Step 1: Gather a small collection of tealights in flameproof holders and arrange in a circle on a table.

Step 2: Sit with a pen and paper and think about what you'd like to release to the flames. This could be something from your past, guilt you have been carrying, or a negative behavior that you'd like to change. It could even be any stress you have experienced from the previous week. Once you have identified something, write a few words to describe what it is on the paper.

Step 3: Light the candles to create a ring of fire, then take the paper and place it in the center of the circle. Say *"I release what I have been carrying, I give it to the flame. The weight is gone, I can now move on."* Breathe deeply and let the power of the words sink in.

Step 4: When you are ready, snuff out each flame but leave one still burning. Fold the paper and pass it through the flame, then let it burn to ash in a fireproof bowl.

Step 5: You might want to scatter the ashes outside as you repeat the words above, or dispose of them some other way.

be kind

Autumn's slower tempo offers us a pause, a time to take stock and consider how we treat ourselves and others. Kindness is an important part of this. Even if you do your best to be kind to others, how kind are you to yourself? Be kind, caring, and full of love—it starts with you.

Sit with your journal and consider the things that make you feel good. A relaxing soak in the bath? Reading a good book? Eating a piece of chocolate? Going to the gym? Listening to your favorite song? In your journal, make a list of all the things that bring you pleasure and then pick one to do each day this week. Don't forget or make excuses. Set the time aside and choose your pleasure. You deserve it!

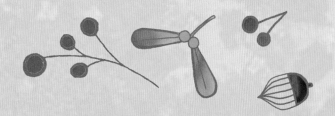

do a kind deed

Make a list of all the things you could do to help someone out. It doesn't matter if the things on your list seem small to you, as they are still important and could make all the difference to someone else. For example, helping someone who is struggling to carry their shopping, giving someone that serves you a kind word or compliment, or popping around to an elderly neighbor to say hello. Include bigger things too, like weeding a neighbor's backyard, volunteering to help at a homeless shelter, or spending some time talking through a problem with a friend. Whatever it is, if it's helping someone out, it counts.

Once you have made your list, go through it and pick one thing that you can do at the weekend. Try to get through everything you have listed and tick things off as you go, so that you can see how well you have done.

But don't worry if that's not possible. These are ideas for the future, and you won't always have the time available. This is not about adding to your stress; it is simply a guide for when you have the space in your life. Hopefully it will remind you to be kind to those you meet, to friends and family, and most of all, to yourself.

MANTRA FOR THE WEEK:

"I treat myself and the world around me with kindness."

forage

As the autumn trees shed their leaves, this natural cycle of letting go provides a treasure trove for the creatures that inhabit the woodland floor.

In the same way, the clutter in your home may also reflect the situation in your head. Often, we hang on to things physically when we are holding on to things emotionally. Getting rid of things is cathartic. It might be hard, but the physical act of shedding can help you feel at peace and ready for your next adventure.

While you may want to eliminate some items from your life to create space, there will be other things that you want to keep close, to remind you of happy times, special memories, and other blessings. For the moments when you need an instant pick-me-up or to restore harmony, create a mobile treasure trove of all the goodness.

make a treasure trove

You will need an old purse or wallet that you can upcycle for this purpose. Go on a hunt for photos, pictures, quotes, ticket stubs, and so on, that remind you of cherished moments. Simple things, like a receipt from a lovely family meal out, will take you back to that time and how you felt. If you prefer, you can write down memories, or just make a quick list of things that you're grateful for and include this. Pop everything inside the purse or wallet and carry it with you.

this week UPCYCLE AND RECYCLE

Go through your wardrobe and consider what you can recycle. A change of season is a great time to do this. Clearing some space will help you see what you have, while donating items you no longer wear or need to charity will generate a positive glow. This is often a time-consuming job, so begin in the week and do a little each day to take you through to the weekend.

Monday: Open your wardrobe door and assess the situation. Imagine that your clothes are living entities. Do they have room to breathe, or are they crammed together? Can you see what is there or do you have to root through to find what you need? This will give you an idea of how much work you need to do.

Tuesday: Go through each item and ask yourself: "Have I worn this in the past year?" and "Will I wear it in the coming year?" Be honest. If the answer is no, then it can go. Make a pile of items that you no longer need.

Wednesday: Donate anything you no longer want to keep by taking any discarded clothing to your local charity store.

Thursday: Go through your wardrobe and thin out what is left by picking garments that you'd only wear in the spring or summer. These can be folded and packed away somewhere safe for next year.

Friday: Assess your wardrobe again. How does the space now make you feel? Are there any items that you still love but no longer wear? Is there anything that can be repurposed or recycled?

At the weekend: This weekend, remember that *"each day is an opportunity to reinvent myself."* Look at some of the items that you didn't donate. Is there a way to repurpose them? Investigate practical things that you can do with old clothes. Tie a few socks together to create a new toy for your dog or cat, or cut up worn, frayed clothes to use as cleaning cloths.

glow and let go

Trees take center stage in autumn as the leaves blaze in fiery, golden and amber hues. This season heralds their moment in the spotlight—and it is the same for you.

As autumn's burnished glow continues to paint the landscape with color, it brings to life features that previously seemed to blend into the background, which you might not have noticed at first glance. It's time for you, too, to acknowledge your greatness—to think about all the many facets that make you special and add to your brightness. Remember that *"every day is an opportunity to value myself even more."*

An important part of self-love is knowing when to move on from something or someone. Whether it's a behavior pattern that no longer serves you, a toxic relationship, a bad situation, or just a feeling of guilt from the past, autumn is the perfect time to cast these situations and relationships aside. Think of it like a tree shedding leaves in time for the winter. As the wheel of nature turns, it offers a chance for renewal. Use the energy of the season to move forward, to find balance, and to gain inner peace.

recognize your worth

Consider your gifts and talents like the leaves that cloak the trees. They are always with you in some form. They grow, they glow, and then they return to the earth, before being reborn in new ways. Bring to mind all the qualities that make you, you. Run through them in your mind at any point during the day, and smile. Know that just like the autumn leaves, you glow!

meditation SHED YOUR LEAVES

This ritual is best performed in the evening, in a moment of calm. Make sure you are alone and that you won't be disturbed during this time.

Step 1: Sit somewhere comfortably and wrap yourself in a blanket so that you feel cozy and secure.

Step 2: Light a white candle to represent peace and healing. Spend a few minutes gazing into the flame of the candle to clear your mind, then close your eyes.

Step 3: Imagine you're standing in forest of trees. It's the middle of autumn, and the air is thick with fog. As you stand, your feet sink into the ground and you can sense tiny threads growing from the soles of your feet and spreading into the earth. These roots anchor you in place. Slowly, steadily, in your mind picture yourself transforming into a tree. Your branches extend outward, and they are covered in golden leaves.

Step 4: Bring to mind the thing that you wish to release from your life. Whatever it is, it is represented by the leaves that cloak you. Say *"I shed my leaves, cast them away. I move toward a bright, new day."* As you take a breath, imagine a huge gust of wind blowing through the forest. This powerful blast of air shakes the leaves from your branches, and they are swept away.

Step 5: Open your eyes and cast off the blanket from your shoulders. Stand and give your limbs a shake to get the blood flowing. Let the candle burn down as you enjoy your newfound sense of inner peace.

daydream

Even if you struggle with artistic pursuits, you can connect with your creative power by doing something that comes naturally to every human on the planet ... and that is daydreaming.

Be decadent and allow yourself a set time to daydream. Don't rush the process. Even if you feel you are wasting your time, daydreaming provides an opportunity for you to relax. If it helps, you might like to sit in front of a window so that you can gaze at the outside world. Let your mind wander and close your eyes if you find that comfortable. You might be surprised by how creative you can be!

Try to see things happening to you and imagine how you would feel. For example, if you've always wanted to learn how to fly, you might picture yourself being the pilot of an airplane, in control and looping through the air. You might feel exhilarated and free in that moment. Enjoy those feelings for what they are, and let the narrative play out in your head.

Continue to harness this innovative energy and work with your journal throughout the week and the coming weekend. Focus on stretching your imagination and allow your creative gifts to shine with these exercises. Use the time on your morning commute, or during your lunch break if you prefer, to unleash your innate creativity. When you use your imagination, you enliven your senses and engage the creative part of the brain, which in turn helps you to feel inspired and hopeful.

this week SET YOUR IMAGINATION FREE

You will need your journal and a pen for this creative exercise.

Monday: Give yourself five minutes to reflect upon your journey to work or your lunchtime walk. Write a short description of what happened. A few sentences describing this is fine.

Tuesday: Today, challenge yourself to write another paragraph. This time, consider each of your senses in turn. Think about what you could see, hear, smell, taste, and touch. Also recall any significant thoughts you had at the time.

Wednesday: Reread the two paragraphs and you should notice that the second description has depth and color and is altogether more engaging. This is because you have brought the scene to life and made it a sensory experience. Recognize your creative streak and let it infuse everything you do for the rest of the day.

Thursday: Next, imagine you could do anything or go anywhere. Let the story flow in your mind and don't restrict yourself. It doesn't matter if your dreams seem far-fetched—this exercise is about stretching your imagination.

Friday: Write a summary of yesterday's daydream in your journal. Recall how you felt during the dream and incorporate as much detail as possible.

At the weekend: Read the creative writing you have produced this week. Think about ways you could recreate those feelings in your life right now. Is there an activity you could do that would help you experience that same sense of freedom? Make a note of any ideas or thoughts that spring to mind.

harvest

Over the past few months, you've learned how to withdraw and slow down, and how to release the past and embrace the elements and the changes within your environment. You've harnessed your creativity and acknowledged your successes. You've also experienced the beauty of stillness and silence. Now you can combine all of these things with a celebration … of yourself!

How do you feel about your own company? Are you happy spending time with yourself, or do you feel the constant need to be with others? Enjoying time alone with only your thoughts for company can be a real pleasure and treating yourself to a day out or a special meal is a great way of celebrating you in all your glory.

As you reflect upon the past year, you'll become aware of your victories, from the little daily wins that make you smile and lift your spirits to much bigger challenges that you have overcome. Even if you struggle to identify a success, you can with some effort train your mind to pay attention to those smaller wins when they occur. As you get into the habit of doing this, you'll begin to notice much bigger wins, and this will instill you with calm confidence for the future.

celebrate your victories

Try making a mental note of things that go well throughout the day and slot them into categories, from fitness and social goals to more personal achievements. For example, walking up three flights of stairs at speed might be a fitness victory, while striking up a conversation with a new colleague would be a social goal. Delegating work where you might normally try to

do it all could be a personal success, while sharing how you feel could be an emotional gold star. At the end of the day, recall each victory and do something small to mark it, from sharing your success with a friend or family member to recording it in your journal.

have a date night

Choose somewhere to go by yourself. Think museums and exhibitions, plays, or festivals. A meal out for one can be an uplifting experience that will give you time to notice the world around you and soak up the atmosphere. You don't have to venture out if you don't want to. If the thought of being seen out alone scares you, try something on a smaller scale, like cooking a posh meal just for yourself at home. Decorate the table as you would if you had guests coming for dinner—and dress up, too!

Enjoy the experience and allow yourself to breathe, reflect, and daydream. The point of this exercise is to embrace your uniqueness and everything you have achieved. So, make sure you feel good inside and out and choose something that you know will be fun and interesting.

As you raise a glass to yourself, say *"I take pride in all of my successes"* and recognize your awesomeness.

chapter 4

WINTER

winter's hush

The wheel of the year turns once more and we find ourselves in the depths of winter. It seems that all is quiet, at least upon the surface. The brittle landscape stirs something primal within us. The sight of the stripped, skeletal earth cuts to the marrow of our bones, and we feel exposed, vulnerable to the onslaught of the elements. It might sound a harsh description, but this season more than any other helps to build upon the inner core of peace we hold inside. What could be more natural than to seek comfort in this stillness, to withdraw, and consolidate?

embrace darkness

Peace at this time is about being bold and brave, delving deep into the shadow side of your personality, just as a tiny vole might migrate to the inner sanctum of the soil. You can find warmth in the treasure you hold within. Winter urges you to step away from the superficial, to disconnect from the world of ten thousand things, and instead make only one thing count—you, and who you really are.

"It is the life of the crystal, the architect of the flake, the fire of the frost, the soul of the sunbeam. This crisp winter air is full of it."

John Burroughs

It is tempting, when faced with the ice and cold, to retreat completely from the world around you. In fact, the key to serenity lies in engaging with your surroundings, opening your heart and mind, and learning to value the beauty of emptiness. The whirlwind of summer has long gone, dragging its older sister autumn by the hand, and now you are left with the silence. This can be scary and there is a temptation to fill the void, but do not be afraid of the darkness that impinges upon your day. The light may be limited, but you will always find a moment of brilliance to counteract the gloom. It is here, in the blank snowy expanse of your surroundings, that you will find true illumination.

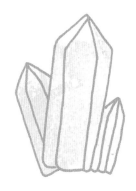

Winter urges you to step into the vista and drink in the cool brightness, feel the chill of the biting wind and the frosty sting of air against skin, and breathe into it. There is nothing dull about this new environment. If you were to wrap up warm and explore, you would understand that there are many magical secrets lurking beneath the surface. Footprints in the snow reveal an array of wildlife on your doorstep, while sugary snowflakes and the frozen imprints of former leaves appear to have been spun out of stardust. Misty, haze-ridden mornings slowly transform into a rich oil painting of a day when anything can happen.

It's time to cozy up with those you love, and show them that you care. But, most of all, it's time to nurture the "you" nestled inside, the part of yourself that others rarely see. Value the gifts of the season and use their bounty to help you rest and recuperate.

go within

On the following pages, you will find suggestions, exercises, and techniques to help you navigate the winter months with tranquility and repose. You will be encouraged to step off the wheel, to recline and readjust the settings on your internal clock. You'll be asked to contemplate what is important to you and why, and to shed superfluous layers, just like the landscape that you find yourself in. Reflection is key, but while there will be many opportunities to relax and ruminate, to take stock and recharge in the toasty warmth of your own haven, there will also be challenges. You'll find that activity features too, and that connecting with others and your environment will help you find clarity and purpose.

Inner peace can come in many forms, and sometimes simply fueling the fire in your belly will give you the momentum and stability you need to float through the day with ease. Winter may appear to be a natural conclusion, but depending on where you are in the world, it doesn't always mean the ending of the year. Changes are afoot even if you can't see them. They are present beneath the shell of the earth, as they are within you. This is the season to uncover those transitions. Reacquaint yourself with what really matters to you and those you care about. Dig deep and you will not only discover the path toward peace, but you will also realize that it has always been there, at the heart of who you are.

WINTER WATCH

If you only do one thing this winter, use the time to reflect on what you care about. What do you value in life, and where do you need to focus your attention? Take inspiration from the landscape, from the trees laid bare and barren, and shed those surface layers made up of superficial things. Instead of worrying about the opinions of others, go to the heart of the question and ask: *"What do I really care about right now?"*

feel festive

As the nights draw in and the temperature drops, use the element of fire to create a ritual that you can enjoy with family and friends.

There's nothing like a roaring fire to help you feel cozy and at peace. Gazing into the flames can provide a focus for the mind, and the soothing heat and comforting, burning crackle make you feel warm and relaxed.

winter elixir

There's nothing like a soothing brew curled up in the warm, to make you feel cozy and nurtured. Winter's bounty is rich in hearty, earthy vegetables and warm spices like nutmeg and cinnamon, which will fire those inner embers and promote a deep sense of peace and comfort.

Ginger, in particular, is a spice that helps to calm digestion, while nutmeg, with its gorgeously nutty aroma, reduces inflammation and helps to prevent blood sugar from spiking. Cinnamon is also packed full antioxidants. Combine all three in a warming elixir that you can enjoy as a mid-morning boost.

Soak a piece of ginger root in a cup of hot water. Allow the root to steep for at least five minutes, then decant the liquid into a fresh cup. Stir with a cinnamon stick and add a pinch of nutmeg. Sip, breathe, and relax.

Enjoy the brew over a good chat—as you connect with others, acknowledge that *"spending time with family and friends soothes my soul."*

this weekend FIRE RITUAL

Fire has been used for centuries as a tool for cleansing and bringing peace and strength. Use this ritual to let go of anything you no longer need, from paperwork to emotional baggage. Make it a sociable event and an excuse to get together with your nearest and dearest. This ritual is best performed outside—build a fire from scratch or use a firepit. But if you really don't want to venture into the cold, you could use a log burner or open fire in your hearth.

Step 1: Create a circle of seats using chairs and cushions so that everyone is comfortable.

Step 2: Build the fire (in your hearth or an outdoor firepit) and gaze into the flames.

Step 3: Make this a time for sharing tales and memories. You might want to talk about the week you've had and ask how people are feeling. If everyone is on board, you could make this a time for sharing your hopes and dreams.

Step 4: Get those gathered to write what they wish for on a piece of paper, and then take it in turns to cast the wishes into the flames. Alternatively, write what you'd like to release on some paper and throw it into the fire.

Step 5: Sit in stillness. While gazing into the embers, draw in the positive energy.

seize the dark

It can be hard to feel positive about the day ahead when you're faced with a dark and gloomy winter morning. We are creatures of the light and we crave the sunshine, but that doesn't mean we can't find a glimmer of peace within the shadows. Instead of lamenting the darkness, embrace it.

It's tempting to want to stay under the duvet on a winter's day. After all, there's little sunshine, the weather is cold, the days are shorter, and you're probably not feeling motivated. If you want to benefit from a good night's sleep, remind yourself to *"follow the natural rhythms of the earth and find my peace."* Follow your circadian rhythms, the body's natural internal cycles that cover a 24-hour period. Here are some top tips to help you feel rested and calm.

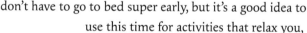

get into good sleep habits

Let the light inspire you. When it starts to brighten outside, take that as your cue to move. It's time to get out of bed and seize the day. Similarly, at night when it begins to get dark, take that as your cue to wind down. You don't have to go to bed super early, but it's a good idea to use this time for activities that relax you, like reading, a scented soak in the bath, watching your favorite TV show, or meditating.

Make sure that throughout your day you get enough exercise. This doesn't mean you have to hit the gym; a leisurely stroll is enough to help settle your rhythms later when you want to sleep.

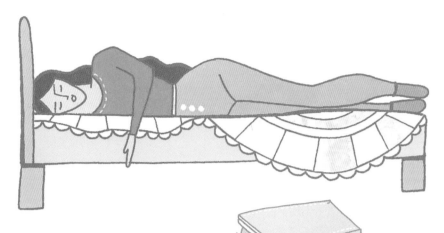

Try to avoid firing up your digestive system, which keeps your body active and awake. Eat your dinner a little earlier than you would normally and resist the urge to snack heavily before bed.

Make sure that your room is neither too hot nor too cold. Snuggling up under layers with the heating on full blast is tempting, but if you can make your bedroom a little cooler than the other rooms in your house, you will benefit because the drop in temperature stimulates relaxation and sleep.

visualization ENCHANTED VEIL

Picture the sky as a warm blanket around your shoulders. Draw it close and imagine that within the murky depths there is magic. You cannot see it. You do not know what it is yet, but as the day develops and the world around you brightens, it will reveal its beauty. Feel the enchantment of this black veil that you draw about you and make a wish. Ask the universe to bless your day in some way. As you exhale, let the wish travel with your breath into the cool morning air. Relax and embrace the calmness within.

cocoon

There's something about being snuggled up that instinctively makes us feel calmer. It's easy to see why we might hanker for this kind of comfort during the winter months.

The cold weather, coupled with the lack of light, calls to our circadian rhythms, while being encased in warmth takes us back to the womb and provides a sense of security that is reassuring. This week, retreat into your own world by creating a cocoon of softness that appeals to all your senses.

Once you're accustomed to the comfort of feeling safe and cocooned, take this up a notch with some self-soothing. Hugs make you feel good (see opposite). They offer a moment of human contact, a tender closeness that helps to settle the body and mind. There will be times when you could do with a hug but there is nobody to hand. That doesn't mean you should go without! Simply remind yourself: *"I self-soothe and unwind every day."* You can feel the benefits from hugging yourself in the safe space that you have created (see page 84).

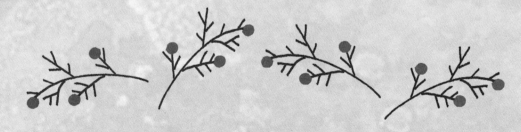

sensory A WARM HUG

Enjoy the deep feelings of comfort that this exercise provides. It only takes a minute, but it's a practice that is instantly calming. You will need a soft and snuggly blanket. Opt for something fleecy and warm in texture, or if you have a favorite blanket from childhood, use that. You'll also want a selection of cushions and some lavender or ylang ylang essential oil (both fragrances have soothing properties). You will also need a piece of rose quartz, either polished or a cluster.

Step 1: Find an area to sit where you won't be disturbed. Arrange the cushions so that they are supporting your back, feet, and head. Add three or four drops of the essential oil to the blanket. Light the candle, then wrap the blanket around you. Make sure it covers your head, so you are completely cocooned. Take a moment to connect with how this feels and to breathe in the comfort.

Step 2: Place the rose quartz either on your lap or between your feet. Take note of the soothing, rosy hue of the stone and imagine that you are bathed from head to toe in the same soft pink glow. Breathe in this healing energy, and as you exhale, imagine you are sending rays of love and light out to the world.

Step 3: Relax in this cocoon of scent, warmth, and color. Know that in this place you are safe and protected from the outside world. You don't have to do or be anything. You can simply breathe and unwind.

Step 4: Sit comfortably and wrap your arms loosely around your body. Place your hands on your upper arms and gently rub them up and down as you hug yourself. Close your eyes and breathe deeply.

hibernate

At this time of year, most of the wildlife in your environment has gone to ground. It's natural for many tiny creatures to hibernate, to rest and recharge beneath the earth, as it helps them stay warm and conserve energy. While you might feel like doing the same, life goes on above the surface.

You can follow suit in a different way. Protect the flora and fauna around you by making sure they are warm and have a safe space. But also make sure that you take inspiration from the animals and plants around you and care for yourself, too.

protect your plants

During the winter, when frosty mornings are rife, it's important to protect the plant life in your backyard. There are some flowers and plants that do not cope well with the cold. Do some investigating, and make sure that the flora in your care is appropriately covered. You can use a thin gauze or some netting which is available in most hardware and garden stores, or alternatively repot those plants that really struggle and bring them inside so that they're protected from extreme frosts.

As you tend to your plants, treat them like friends. Be kind and gentle and focus solely on what you are doing. Be present and in the moment while you are looking after them, as this will help to generate positive and calming energy that benefits both you and the natural world.

curl up

Start every day feeling calm and balanced by bringing your center of gravity down to the ground. Take inspiration from the furry mammals, who seek refuge beneath the earth at this time of year, and snuggle up on the floor. Make this a part of your waking-up ritual so that you get into the habit of starting your day feeling centered.

Begin in a kneeling position, with your back straight and your shoulders back. Take a deep breath in, and as you exhale, lower yourself forward so that your forehead brushes the floor. Wrap your hands around the top of your head, so that you're all curled up and your forearms touch the floor.

You should feel comfortable and relaxed in this position. Breathe deeply and nestle. Take comfort from being close to the earth and hold this position for at least a minute. Slowly uncurl yourself and rock back until you are kneeling again.

MANTRA FOR THE WEEK:

"I am a part of nature, and nature is a part of me."

visualization BENEATH THE SURFACE

Take hibernation inspiration from your cozy animal friends—make sure you won't be disturbed, by switching off your phone and any other form of technology, and go beneath the surface of your mind with this soothing meditation.

Step 1: Relax and get comfortable. Close your eyes and to begin with focus on your breathing. Pay attention to the gentle rise and fall of your chest. Notice the journey of each breath, as you inhale deeply and feel your lungs inflate. Notice, too, how it feels to gradually release the breath, letting it slip between your lips.

Step 2: Count the beats of each breath and extend your outer breath by an extra count. Really hold on to the air as long as you can. Feel the oxygen fuel your body and calm your mind.

Step 3: Now imagine you are cocooned deep in the belly of the earth. You can sense the soil against your skin, softly nourishing you. You can sense the blanket of the earth above your head. You can feel plant roots curling around your body and supporting you. They hold you in place loosely, allowing you to breathe and feel safe. There is nothing to fear here, you are at one with nature, and you can harness this energy to help you feel balanced and strong.

Step 4: You breathe in. You breathe out. You enjoy the warmth and security. Let any thoughts pass through your mind, and if anything strikes you as important, you can come back to it later. Use this space to reflect and recharge.

Step 5: When you're ready, focus once more on your breathing. Count the beats of each inhalation and exhalation, and again notice the rise and fall of your chest. Gently open your eyes and give your body a shake and a stretch, before leaping into action.

nest

In winter we can create a kind of nest in our homes, which offers us protection and strength. From this place of sanctuary, you can see the world outside, shielded in your hiding place. Here you are at peace, able to center yourself and appreciate the wonders of nature.

The wildlife in your backyard also needs a place to retreat and find some comfort from winter's chill. Give the creatures that share your world a helping hand by creating a habitat that is perfect for them to survive and thrive during the colder months.

If you have lots of excess leaves, instead of getting rid of them, sweep them up into a large pile. This is the ideal environment for insects and other tiny creatures and bugs to snuggle down in. Fallen branches also make an excellent shelter for hedgehogs, chipmunks, and other small mammals, so add them to the bundle you've created. Spread some of the leaves over your backyard borders. Over time they will form a mulch, which is a great food source for foraging blackbirds. Also, resist the urge to chop down seedheads and cut back stems. They might not look pretty, but they're a great place for ladybugs to settle over winter.

Clean all your bird feeders and position them ready for purpose. Fill them with seeds and nuts but remember also to scatter some on the ground as larger birds like blackbirds and thrushes will benefit from this.

this week PROTECT GARDEN FRIENDS

Our garden friends, like hedgehogs and other garden creatures, need a helping hand during the winter months when they are looking for a safe, warm space to hibernate. Give something back to the environment by creating a hibernation box that they can use during winter.

A garden sanctuary doesn't have to be elaborate. You can repurpose items to create the perfect nature-friendly haven. If you don't have hedgehogs in your neighborhood, that's fine as the box doesn't have to be specific to any creature. Treat it as a "hibernation hotel" for small mammals like chipmunks or squirrels that might need somewhere to hunker down over the winter months. As long as you include plenty of straw, dry grass, and earthy material, and position it somewhere out of the way, they'll be happy to use it.

Monday: Find a suitable space in your backyard for the box. Somewhere shady and quiet, either near a hedge or behind a shed, would be ideal. Make sure the entrance is out of the wind so that the creature inside can stay toasty warm.

Tuesday: Source your materials. Start by making a list of the things you will need to create your box. A plastic storage box makes a good home, as does a decent-sized planter. If you're using a planter, you might want to clear it out first. You will also need an abundance of leaf litter, twigs, and soil for the bedding and to disguise the box or planter.

Wednesday: Set to work creating the box. Cut or drill a small entrance at the front and add some breathing holes around the sides.

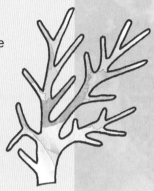

Thursday: Position the box in its location and begin to build up the bedding inside. Layer the leaves on top of each other with twigs and soil to create a comfy mattress for any creature that stops by for a snooze. You can also use pet straw to build this up. When this is complete, use excess soil and twigs to disguise the box and help it to fit in with its surroundings.

Friday: Look at the rest of your backyard, and make sure it's accessible to your wildlife friends. Think about how these creatures are going to get into your backyard. Ensure there are small spaces between hedges and borders, or small holes or gaps in garden, that they can pass through easily and leave small piles of soil and twigs around to encourage them in.

At the weekend: Consider other animals and small birds, and what you can do to help them. For example, build an insect hotel by piling up pine cones, leaving tiny spaces between the cones and covering them with leaves.

see the sparkle

There is nothing more awe-inspiring or peaceful than a snowy scene. When all around is covered in a blanket of white, it's as if the earth is muffled. Sound is swallowed and all that remains is a glistening vista of brightness.

sensory TAKE A PICTURE

This exercise is about appreciating what you see and capturing the uniqueness of the moment. In doing so, you give your imagination room to breathe. You step outside of yourself and your worries and find a different kind of peace through the sense of vision. The more you practice this kind of "seeing," the more you'll notice the wonder in everyday vistas, which in turn promotes the flow of harmony in your life.

Step 1: Step outside for a moment and breathe. Take in the landscape. It doesn't matter whether you are in a city, on your street, or in a backyard, just stop and do a 180-degree scan of the area. Does anything catch your eye? If so, home in on it. Perhaps you're drawn to tree or a well-worn bench that happens to be in your line of view, or maybe the shape of a roof or a particular clump of clouds make an interesting pattern.

Step 2: Imagine increasing your focus so that the object of your attention becomes bigger. Picture a frame around it that highlights the shape and structure, all the edges and curves, the color and brightness. Take in as much detail as you can and take a picture with your eyes.

Step 3: As you study the object, words or feelings may spring to mind (if they don't, that's fine too). If they do, write a description in your journal.

MANTRA FOR THE WEEK:

"I find my balance in the natural world."

If you're lucky enough to find yourself standing at the center of this kind of landscape, or any other beautiful scene, take a minute to just watch. Remind yourself to ***"see, feel, and experience wonder at my surroundings."*** There will always be something within the picture that is special and unique to the time of year. Whether you're an avid people watcher, or you just like to stare out of the window, the joy of watching life go on around you while doing absolutely nothing is revitalizing. It allows you to completely switch off but still be active and entertained by your environment. You can breathe in the silence and let the tingle of icy coolness soothe body, mind, and soul.

be a watcher

Engage your imagination and let a narrative unfold. For example, you might sit in the park at lunchtime and notice a young girl with an elderly couple feeding the ducks. You might guess that these are her grandparents and that they're having a fun day out. Slowly the story takes shape, as you become the viewer of this special moment in their life. Watching the world go by for just a few minutes each day will help you see the bigger picture, reframe your focus, and enjoy a moment of tranquility in your busy schedule.

winter wonderland

Even at the heart of the season there will be days that are more dreary than dreamy, but there's nothing like a wintery scene to calm the soul and make you appreciate the beauty of the natural world.

If you remain aware of your surroundings as you go about your business, you will notice small things that add color and value to your day. You will also benefit from the peace that comes from being present and in the moment. Go into each day with the mindset that you are going to slow down time and make the most of every minute.

slow down time

Stop for one minute—set the alarm on your phone to sound when the minute is up.

During this time, close your eyes and breathe deeply. Don't try to anticipate when the alarm will sound, simply enjoy the peace that this moment of quiet time provides. You will probably be surprised by how long the minute lasts.

Repeat this exercise three or four times during the day. This will help you relax and disengage from the outside world, and also give you an idea of how long a minute really is.

The next time you are rushing to complete any kind of task, take a deep breath and remind yourself that each minute counts—and lasts much longer than you imagine. Take your time and do what you can.

this weekend CREATE A LIFE-SIZED SNOW GLOBE

If you've not been blessed with a covering of snow this winter, you can create a similar feeling by making your home into a snow globe. To get into the spirit, you'll need lots of pretty crystals, twinkling lights that you can hang around your home, snowy white pillows, throws, and blankets, and white and silver candles or tealights.

Step 1: Choose an area to decorate, such as your living room, and set about making it look as magical and wintry as possible. Cover old sofas with white throws and blankets and scatter fluffy white pillows on the floor and chairs.

Step 2: Arrange candles and tealights at various positions throughout the room and light them. Place clusters of quartz crystals together to catch the twinkling light. If you have a wreath of lights that you can drape from the ceiling or along the walls in some way, do this. Snow globes are a beautiful way to recreate a miniature wonderland. If you have one to hand, give it a shake and watch as the snow falls.

Step 3: Once you have set a scene of serenity, sit or stand at the center and breathe in the atmosphere. Imagine that outside the snow has fallen, and you are safe and warm within this wintry haven.

expand your horizons

This winter, make a point of tapping into your higher self, and allow your intuition to be your guide.

When you're in tune with your intuition, you are in sync with your body and mind and connected to the world. You are in the flow and instinctively able to tap into your higher self, the subconscious part of your mind that always has your best interests at heart. This level of connection provides a deep sense of peace and well-being. Instead of fretting about the future, or letting anxiety govern your thoughts, you'll feel more centered, and you will be able to see the signs and synchronicities at work in your life.

broaden your bookshelf

Nothing beats curling up with a good book. It's a restorative practice that can help you unwind and find a moment of peace at any point during the day. Instead of reaching for the same type of book to chill with, broaden your horizons and go for something completely different. If you're a thriller lover, you might choose a feel-good rom com. If you're a fan of fantasy, you could try a non-fiction memoir of someone you admire. Be bold and switch things up with your reading matter. You'll not only stimulate the mind, but you'll also appreciate the stillness that can be found in doing things differently.

sensory GO BAREFOOT

We often underestimate the sense of touch. Experiencing the touch of something different can introduce us to new experiences and open new vistas. It is also extremely comforting and can be used to calm and soothe. Your feet have been doing the hard work of carrying you forward through each season, so it's time they had a sensory treat.

Step 1: Fill a large bowl with warm water, add a drop of your favorite bath oil or bubbles, and position on the floor near a fluffy mat or rug.

Step 2: Remove your shoes and socks and massage each foot gently to get the circulation going. Use your thumb in a circular movement around the ball of the foot and over the top.

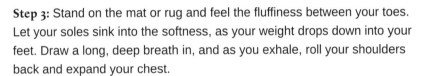

Step 3: Stand on the mat or rug and feel the fluffiness between your toes. Let your soles sink into the softness, as your weight drops down into your feet. Draw a long, deep breath in, and as you exhale, roll your shoulders back and expand your chest.

Step 4: When you're ready, sit down and place your feet in the bowl of water. Close your eyes and focus on the sensation of the warm liquid as it surrounds and cushions each foot. Wiggle your toes and let your feet play in the water. Breathe deeply and enjoy those feelings of peace and comfort.

plentiful mindset sticky notes

Write on a handful of sticky notes: *"My higher self guides and protects me."*
Know that you have all the answers within you. When you shift focus and act
from a higher mindset, you will always do the best for yourself and others.
Go on a journey through your home, thinking about the key places you visit
during the day, such as the bathroom mirror first thing in the morning.
Position the sticky notes in these places, and every time you see them,
repeat the affirmation out loud or in your head.

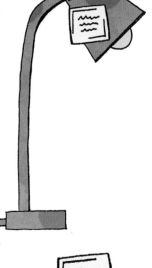

speak to your higher self

Imagine there's a speech bubble coming out of the top of your head. This
space is your "higher self," and it is here that you find ideas, inspiration,
and thoughts that urge you to act in a certain way. Spend a few minutes
visualizing this bubble and let any thoughts flow into your mind.

When you need a little guidance from your intuition, place
your hands on the area above your navel. This is known as
the solar plexus and is the seat of your emotions. Notice
how this space feels and take your cue from that.

Look for signs that come out of the blue. For example,
if you keep hearing the same words in conversation, on
the radio, in a song, or in a book, take note and recognize
that this could be a message from your intuition. There
is a reason why these words resonate with you—your
intuition is guiding you.

be enough

It may be cold outside, it may be gloomy, but that's no excuse to slip into
a scarcity mindset. Silence the inner critic whenever it raises its head, by
actively reminding yourself that you are enough and that you have enough.
You have everything you need in your life, right now.

keep warm

This season encourages you to nurture yourself. Put self-care and love at the top of your list.

Looking after your needs can be something as simple as wrapping up warm before you leave the house. Revel in the softness of your winter hat and scarf and snuggle between layers of chunky knits. These are practical things, but they are the basis of self-care at this time of year. Nurturing your needs is about feeding your body and mind with love. Hugs, too, are good for you—and the person you're hugging! Don't be afraid to hug yourself when you need it (see page 116).

meditation **FEEL THE LOVE**

Any time you're feeling vulnerable and in need of a calm moment, try this exercise to soothe yourself and experience inner peace.

Step 1: Think back to how your day has gone. Were there any moments that you found difficult? Perhaps you feel tense because of a stressful situation. If so, be brave and bring it to mind.

Step 2: See yourself in that moment, dealing with that issue or person. If it's an ongoing problem, reflect on how it started and see yourself at that point. Picture where you were and what you were doing in your head.

Step 3: Now imagine giving that version of you a hug. Wrap your arms around that image and let the love flow from your heart.

Step 4: Tell the imaginary version of yourself that everything will be fine. Say **"I love you"** in your mind, then relax and let the moment slip away.

shadows

As the light dims in the world, it encourages you to go within and face your shadow self. In doing so, you will release any negative emotions and redress imbalance in your life, which helps to restore inner peace.

It sounds scary, but it's important to remember that the shadow self is just another part of you, and like any other aspect of your personality, you are

this week MEET YOUR SHADOW SELF

Embrace every part of yourself to feel acceptance and the inner peace that comes with it. You'll need a pen and your journal for this exercise.

Monday: Prepare a relaxing atmosphere where you can sit and reflect over the following days.

Tuesday: During a quiet moment, bring to mind any negative beliefs or opinions that you have about yourself. For example, you might say "I am not pretty enough" or "I am not clever enough." Write these statements in your journal. You'll know when you've hit on a key aspect of your shadow self because it will strike a chord and feel upsetting to see it written down.

Wednesday: Look at each of the statements you wrote yesterday and consider its truth. Where does it come from? Did someone tell you this directly or is it something you intrinsically feel? Being aware that it's a belief you have adopted will help to banish any negative thought patterns or behaviors associated with it. When you question these beliefs, you will often find that there is no validity to them. Know that while you are aware of the beliefs you carry, this does not make them true. They are simply thoughts you have decided to keep and you can let them go at any point.

Thursday: Get into the habit of questioning yourself and your emotions in your journal. Be specific and ask yourself: "What do I feel right

in control. Your shadow self is controlled by beliefs and patterns of thinking that you have developed over time, and it is these that fuel your darker side.

Every day we experience painful feelings, from trivial frustrations that escalate, to anger at ourselves and the world around us, to fear that gnaws away inside. Sometimes we acknowledge these dark emotions and sometimes we try and swallow them, keeping them hidden from the light. It's important that when these emotions arise, you let them come to the surface. Trying to keep a lid on things will only add to the discomfort and destroy your personal peace. Do not be afraid of what you are feeling.

now?", "Why do I feel this way?" and "Is there anything I can do about it?" If the answer to the final question is "no," then relax and breathe into the emotion. Sit with it and eventually, like free-flowing water, it will travel through you. Place your hands on your heart, breathe in, breathe out, and let the serenity of acceptance fill you up.

Friday: If you could go back in time, what would you tell your younger self? What advice would you give? And how much kinder would you be to that version of you than you are right now to the you of adulthood? Let's be honest, we can be our own harshest critics. If you want to develop a well of inner peace, it's important to learn to be kind, to let go of past mistakes, and to

truly love yourself. Start with the child you once were and let them know just how amazing they are. You will find that once you let those caring sentiments flow, you will feel the benefits in your mood and well-being.

At the weekend: In your journal, compose a beautiful letter to your younger self. Think about the person you were then and the person you are now. What would you love to say to that little child, to help them feel better and navigate the world around them? If ever you need a moment to recharge, and a little loving boost, take your journal out and read through it. Know that you did your best, that you are still doing your best, and that is enough.

feed body and mind

At this time of year, it's important to stay nourished. You might not always feel like heading out for a run or to the gym if it is cold, but there are lots of things you can do at home to take care of your body.

Exercise is one of the best ways to clear your head and feel at peace within yourself. If you combine movement with visualization, you'll get the most out of any exercise, and also enhance the benefits that you feel.

The food you eat can help you maintain a healthy immune system, while also keeping your mind in tip-top shape. Try to eat seasonally, and include lots of fresh fruit, vegetables, pulses, and plant-based foods in your diet. At the weekend you'll have the time to plan ahead, and even prep some meals for the following week, so don your apron and work a little kitchen magic to soothe body and mind.

sweep away the cobwebs

A sweep of your front path to clear away any debris or snow that has gathered is a great way to get your body moving. Breathe deeply as you go and put energy into each movement. Imagine that with each sweep, you are clearing away self-doubt, anxiety, and any other negative thoughts in your mind. The same can be said for vacuuming or mopping within the home. Use the action and the intention to bring clarity and clean away all those nagging doubts and fears.

this weekend SOUP FOR THE SOUL

Soups are easy to cook in advance and they're super nutritious. You can use up an enormous amount of leftover vegetables and add extra protein with pulses like lentils and barley.

Step 1: Collect together a large cooking pot, a hand-blender, lots of tasty vegetables, around 3 cups (25fl oz/ 700ml) of hot water or stock, and some salt and pepper to enhance the flavor.

Step 2: To begin, chop up the vegetables into smaller pieces of roughly the same size. Finely chop an onion.

Step 3: Add a little olive oil to the pot and fry the onion, then add the other vegetables.

Step 4: Add the water. Let the mixture cook down and simmer. Keep adding a little water so that it doesn't dry out and you have plenty of liquid. You will need to cook this for about an hour, but it will be worth it as you'll get more from the taste and it will be easier to blend.

Step 5: Add some salt and pepper and any other herbs that you fancy. Then take the pan off the stovetop and use the blender to create a smooth, soup-like consistency.

Step 6: At this point, have a taste and adjust the seasoning. You might want to add a little cream if you'd like a richer soup.

Step 7: Serve with your favorite bread or salad. If you're cooking in advance, you can wait until the mixture has cooled, portion it into containers, and freeze.

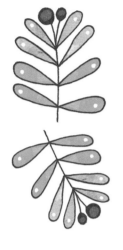

release the past

Winter urges us to dig deep, to reflect on past grievances, and forgive wholeheartedly in order to create an inner well of serenity.

Forgiveness is a quality that is often underrated, but important if you want peace of mind. Some believe it is weak to forgive, when in fact it takes a degree of strength and courage to look back, address those painful moments, and then let them go. Remind yourself to *"find serenity in forgiving myself and others."* Forgiveness comes in many shapes and forms, and it can be most effective when you use it on yourself. Sometimes we find it easier to feel compassion for others than to forgive ourselves for something we have done.

step back and count to ten

There will be points during your day that you will encounter tension in some form. Perhaps someone has upset you and you feel angry. This is perfectly reasonable, and you're allowed to feel that way. Rather than overreacting in the moment and causing both you and the other person even more stress, take a step back and give yourself a moment to breathe.

Physically, if you can, take a step backward, putting you at a distance from the person or thing that has unsettled you. At this point, take a deep breath in, and as you exhale slowly, count to ten. Do this in a steady, gradual rhythm. By the time you reach the number ten in your mind, you should feel much calmer and able to react with judgment.

meditation EMBRACE FORGIVENESS

Be brave and bring forgiveness into your life using these simple steps.

Step 1: To begin, make sure you feel calm and compassionate. Create a loving atmosphere by making sure you are comfortable and relaxed. Bring to mind the situation, person, or issue that has caused you pain. Instead of reliving every moment, simply acknowledge what happened and talk to the person in your mind, explaining why you were so hurt.

Step 2: If you can, close your eyes and visualize yourself standing face to face in a circle of light. If you are the person that you need to forgive, then imagine you are alone in the circle. Breathe deeply, and when you are ready, say **"I forgive you."** Place your hands on your heart as you speak the words and feel them.

Step 3: At this point, if you are forgiving another person, you might want to picture them slowly fading from the circle. If the forgiveness is for you, then you might want to imagine yourself becoming lighter, freer, and lifting off the ground like a feather.

Step 4: Repeat the words: **"I forgive you."** When you are ready, open your eyes, breathe, and relax.

live in the moment

While you bear witness to the darkness of winter, do not lament the passing of spring. Instead, live in the moment and adapt to the conditions of your environment. Nature does this seamlessly as it moves through each season.

Experience the present for what it is. In doing so, you will generate positive energy and feel a contentment that will carry you through the coming weeks.

this weekend LEAVE A LIGHT ON

Take a moment to appreciate the gifts of the season and to welcome the return of the light by performing a simple candle ritual.

Step 1: Wait till the evening draws in. Leave your shades open to embrace the darkness and position your favorite candle on the windowsill. Sit and gaze at the scene before you. Look through the window into the blanket of the night and accept that you cannot see everything. The shadows are filled with mystery and promise.

Step 2: Look at the candle in your window. Notice how the flickering flame weaves and dips. It creates a warm glow that brings a coziness to your surroundings. The outside may look grim, but the light in the window offers some illumination.

Step 3: Consider the light within you, and how it grows and dances like the flame of the candle. Sometimes the flame appears small, almost ready to be extinguished. Perhaps the events of the day or the weight of worry becomes too much, and it feels like the shadows are about to engulf you. Then you take a deep breath and suddenly the flame billows and blossoms. In these moments, the world looks brighter and there is beauty to be found. Hold this image in your mind.

Step 4: Know that the spring is coming, but for now you are content to enjoy the

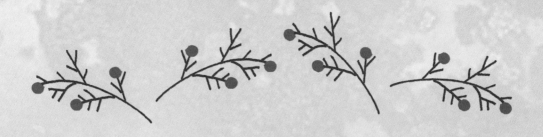

*"The light within me burns bright,
even in the darkest moments."*

blessings of winter. Look at the darkness beyond your window once more. Feel the unknown and open your heart and mind to it. Know that you are safe and protected by the light. Breathe deeply and let the flame within grow to new heights as the candle on your windowsill burns down.

Step 5: Consider your inward breath as the "present" and your outward breath as the "past." Once the breath filters from your body, it is gone, and you are ready to embrace a new breath. Adopt the same approach to those feelings that unsettle you.

Step 6: Cut to a new scene by clapping your hands, or if you prefer, stamping your foot loudly, to mark the end of these past

thoughts, feelings, and experiences. Then take a breath, and as you exhale, know that the moment has passed and positive change is already on its way to you.

the passage to peace

Peace is timeless, ageless, and without limits or boundaries. It is so often sought but seldom found in the world of ten thousand things. It is only when you go within, traversing the corners and rarely trodden avenues of the mind, that you find the holy grail of tranquility. Even then, the hard-won prize of inner peace may slip through your fingers, but there is no need to panic, lament its loss, or tighten your grip in an attempt to hold on to it. Peace still lives within you; it is a matter of preserving it. Remind yourself to take care throughout the year, make time for your well-being, perform the necessary rituals and ministrations that work for you, and provide all the things you need to create a calm environment.

Peace is personal. It is priceless, but unlike other treasured gems, it is always in abundance if you know where to look. Hopefully the seasonal suggestions within these pages have inspired and highlighted some of the things you can do to restore peace and improve the flow of harmony that you experience on a weekly basis. But this is just the first step. Peace is a lifelong journey that you must take alone. That doesn't mean that you are on your own—quite the opposite. Peace can be found within the company of others and in seeking out new friendships. It can be

experienced in a moment of stillness shared with the one you love, or in a solitary instant when it is just you and your thoughts under the cover of silence.

Peace is the ship and you are the captain. The waters you navigate and the way you do this are your decision. There is no map when it comes to inner calm, but that doesn't mean you cannot look for guidance from the universe and the natural world. Sometimes, it helps to try different techniques until you find the one (or several) that fit your lifestyle and then you can develop your own way of doing things. Take what you can from the weekly rituals and suggestions and discard the ideas that don't gel with your thinking. If something piques your interest in this sea of self-soothing, see it as an island and jump ship for a while. A little diversion could be exactly what you need to find your inner haven. Most of all, follow your heart, for it is your emotions that power you through turbulent waters and also provide an anchor to hold you in place, when the need arises. *Bon voyage!*

MANTRA FOR THE YEAR:

"I am in control of my future;
I manifest a life of love and peace."

index

acknowledgments

I would like to thank the wonderful team at CICO publishing who worked hard to bring this book to life. Special thanks go to Kristy Richardson, who helped organize my thoughts and musings in a way that everyone can understand, and to Carmel Edmonds for embracing this idea in the first place. A year is a long time, and it's easy to skip through the seasons without noticing the changes, but this book hopefully provides some food for thought, ideas to nurture peace and love, and practical ways to make positive changes.

resources

Davies, Alison, *How to Find Your Happy Place* (Pyramid, 2022).

Davies, Alison, *The Little Book of Happiness: Live. Laugh. Love.* (Quadrille Publishing Ltd, 2018)

Verni, Ken A. (editor), *Practical Mindfulness: A Step-by-Step Guide* (DK Books, 2015)

Wax, Ruby, *A Mindfulness Guide for Survival* (Welbeck Publishing Group, 2021)

mindfulness.com
a free app with meditations for better sleep and improved health.

calm.com
a useful app for sleep, meditation, and soothing the mind.

insighttimer.com
a meditation app for breathwork, anxiety, and mindfulness